Into Happy Havens
(2nd edition)

All places where the eye of Heaven rests,
Are to a wise man,
Ports and HAPPY HAVENS.

William Shakespeare, Richard 2nd
(1564-1616)

This book is dedicated to the memory of
Judith ,a.k.a. Darling,
My wife of 57 years, who died in 2012.
She lives on in the memory of our 3
children, Sue, Bob & Simon
many friends, family and patients.

INDEX

Chapter 1	THE PUNTERS	page 3
Chapter 2	THE HAPPY PANTRY	page 18
Chapter 3	STRIP POKER	page 25
Chapter 4	PINKY & PERKY	page 43
Chapter 5	THE WEDDING PARTY	page 61
Chapter 6	THE DINNER DATE	page 69
Chapter 7	CASINO CHIPS	page 76
Chapter 8	CONFRONTATION	page 94
Chapter 9	THE SEMINAR	page 124
Chapter 10	THE TRAP	page 149
Chapter 11	SUMO!	page 162
Chapter 12	THE TSO	page 181
Chapter 13	AFTER THE BALL WAS OVER	page 195
Chapter 14	THE WRECKING CREW	page 206
Chapter 15	THE ASSIGNMEENT	page 213
Chapter 16	RETRIBUTION	page 231
Chapter 17	REVENGE	page 236
Chapter 18	REGRET	page 240
Chapter 19	REMORSE	page 244
Chapter 20	REVIEW	page 255
Chapter 21	REBUKE	page 259
Chapter 22	REALITY	page 264
Chapter 23	REFORM	page 277
Chapter 24	RECUPERATION	page 297

CHAPTER 1 The Punters

Most people assume that hotel managers possess a certain *je ne sais quoi* which sets them apart from other managers.

This misleading perception is encouraged by program makers who portray hotel managers as glamorous and heroic leaders of courteous hospitality teams, as smooth, suave diplomats who mix freely with the rich powerful and glamorous denizens of an imaginary cosmopolitan meritocracy which merges seamlessly into realms of luxury, power and status.

Stark reality murders dreams quite casually, and I had to admit that my present circumstances did not allow much room for glamour. In midwinter outer London is a sombre place, far removed from the glitz and sunshine of a cosmopolitan Shangri-La. In my hotel the priorities are closer to sheep herding than hospitality.

Seen from the outside, looking in, my ultramodern hotel set a little back from a busy London ring road was not conspicuous nor did it stand out as a natural focal point for tired travellers.

It lacked the clear-cut identity that those thoughtful designers can graft onto palaces and prisons, banks and battleships. By day, the hotel was not very different from its high-rise office block neighbours standing almost to attention in rank and file on both sides of the wide and busy road. But after sunset on a bleak winter evening it took on a new identity, courtesy of the lighting wizards who could defy darkness with moving dazzle. Suddenly the hotel became as bright as a new beacon, a guiding light for weary travellers from afar, a neon lit lane leading to a peaceful backwater away from the main stream.

Most of the guests [known to the hotel staff as punters] arrived by car and sought a single room with bath. Some punters came by coach, usually as part of a package tour.
They shared rooms. From this simple division flows the relative profitability of modern hotels. Shared rooms are good. Unshared rooms aren't.

The attraction of suburban hotels was free parking for all. As a bonus, the tariff was cheaper than city centre hotels which offered the same facilities but charged extra for parking cars. The significance of reduced cost was not lost on the corporate clients who kept their employees on the move. The front hall was full of punters eager to relax after a day of stress in other parts of London. A long queue trailed from the Reception Desk. More than One hundred punters were already booked in. An unknown number would follow. Most of the punters knew exactly what to do. No welcome speech was necessary. They checked in, signed the registration forms, went to their rooms and got in touch with loved ones, bosses or mates. So, from a busy well-lit Hall the regular punters fanned out all over the Hotel. Most of them became immersed in daily reports. They worried about Sales quotas, their competitors and progress to date. They plugged their laptops into our dedicated terminals and received news, intelligence, orders and omens from afar. They shared today's events with colleagues everywhere. They rehearsed Tomorrow's appointments with joy or dread. They really looked forward to going home on Friday.

It was not the sort of hotel to send a postcard from. The visit was brief and businesslike. It was not memorable. Within the hour, nearly all the bedroom lights were on. In the adjacent buildings, nearly all the lights went out.

From the inside, looking out, a different picture emerged.

"Miss Tammond. Miss Tammond, there's a punter out 'ere wants to see you".

Ethel, my Front Office receptionist, delivered this message. She stood framed in the doorway of my office. A slight elfin figure dressed in the standard grey uniform of our employer, Happy Haven Hotels.

The message was innocent enough, and spoken in the flat Cockney monotone of a true Londoner, charmingly embellished with dropped aitches and a glottal stop that even Hottentots would admire.

This had the effect of changing my gender. The notice on my lapel badge reads Martin Hammond, General Manager.

But that gender switch alone was not enough to account for the rising wave of panic which the message produced. After all, why shouldn't a guest of Happy Haven Hotels want to see me at 6.30 p.m. at the end of a busy day?

My employers, Happy Haven Hotels, are in the business of accommodating travellers in their hotels, which are located in every significant city suburb in the land.
The trade mark of hospitality, [our logo, they call it] is a round orange face wearing a huge smile from ear to ear topped off by eyes screwed up in ecstasy.

The logo is known affectionately as Walter. Although we have not met yet, I do know that Walter is the given name of our esteemed founder - an egomaniac blusterer and modern version of Genghis Khan, focused enough to start another Great Fire of London and blessed with the tunnel vision of a reversed telescope.

His backers and bankers do not share Walter's reputation for ferocity within his empire. He is well known, respected and admired in established financial circles for his ability to repay loans in less than the contracted period. In purely fiscal terms, he is the Right Stuff.

Walter is everywhere. He is on the rotating, illuminated sign outside every hotel. He is on the handle of the door that lets you in. He is on the reservation form that you sign. He smiles at you from free pens and he beams at you from the receptionist's badge that adorns her left breast and reveals her name. He is on the menu in the lift that lists the goodies on tonight's menu. He is on the key swipe to your room and when you get inside he peeps at you from curtains, towels and bedspreads.

By a strange omission, he is not on the loo paper, but he comes back at you almost immediately from the miniature cakes of soap which are laid out with precision beside the wash-hand basin.

Walter is to be admired for his persistence. A characteristic which does not pass unnoticed by his City backers. If you read from the embossed folder in your room you will discover that he can accommodate you in 55 different locations of his own. He can refer you to hundreds more all over the globe if you are a bona fide fare-paying traveller. If you move, Walter can accommodate you when you stop moving, anywhere, anytime.

Walter is all around you, smiling his huge smile, inviting all to sleep blissfully in his rooms. "Comfortable rooms, all with their own en-suite facilities". A euphemism for your very own loo, warranted as unsullied by the asses of over zealous Rugby Football players, local harlots or visiting Arabs-"All rooms have their own private entertainment channels" the adverts scream in upper case, pinning their hopes on the knowledge that if you already possess such advanced consumer goodies you know exactly how to use them. And if you don't, well, it will be fun finding out just what private entertainment channels are and when it shows up alarmingly on your bill, you will be too mortified to query it.

So what is significant about a guest of Walter wanting to see me at 6.30 p.m.? After all I am the manager here, this is *my* hotel. I am at the disposal and pleasure of all Walter's guests throughout the day and night. I am ever ready to oblige or please, to be of service in some helpful small way. To make their stay at a Happy Haven eventful or memorable. To establish a bond of goodwill and courtesy. To extend the boundaries of hospitality into new and untried realms, etc, etc.

And to prop up this impossible corporate dream I was appointed a whole year ago, at the tender age of 27 to manage this monolith. I am the bye-product of a technological age of thrusting go-getters, attuned to modern management techniques, imbued with social consciousness, versed in political manipulation and correctness, a reformed Renaissance Man affiliated to the Tenderness Tendency, a dedicated Team Player with impeccable credentials. And with one over-riding virtue that sets me apart. I cost much less than an experienced manager.

Ethel, still framed in the doorway of my office, assumed my lack of attention was caused by deafness.

"Miss Tammond" she said "there's a punter out 'ere wants to see you."

Ten decibels louder this time and tinged with amusement. The way you speak to the elderly, or foreigners.

"Tell him" I said "that I will be with him immediately".

The guest reception areas of Walter's hotels are always eye catching. Generous in proportion,

appointed to the highest standards, they are designed to be customer friendly.
With just the correct amount of conspicuous consumption.. They are also designed to be capable of herding guests in and out of the revolving front door faster than a dedicated Sheepdog.

It was not difficult to know which guest wanted to see me. When people are angry, they send out very strong vibrations. After meeting the first few hundred you develop an almost clinical interest in the symptoms.
Facial colour somewhere between pale and puce. Eyebrows down and together. Small, straight lines where the mouth should be. Automatic gain on the vocal chords. Nervous tics and body spasms. This guest had all the symptoms. He nearly tripped over his luggage when he saw me.

"Are you the manager"?
"Yes, sir, can I - "
"That girl over there tells me I haven't got a room here."
"I'm sure I can -"
"I rang up from my office last Monday and booked a room here. When I arrived I was told that I haven't got one."
"Well, sir, you see..."
"What is the point in ringing up to book a room if when you get here you are told that you haven't got one?"
"The reservation system here is - "
"Bloody useless." He was on full gain already.

One of the symptoms of irate guests is their willingness to complete sentences for you.

"Happy bloody Haven Hotels are only too pleased to take my money and charge me exorbitant prices for rooms all the year round, but when I arrive here I am told that I haven't got one."

It was beginning to shape up like one of those conversations beloved of political interviewers of the Torquemada school who like to ask the questions and then answer the questions without assistance from their interviewee.

"I am sure that I can explain..."
"I mean, if I go to all the trouble of ringing you up to let you know that I am coming; you would think that common courtesy, common courtesy, would make any ordinary, decent, decent person, get in touch with me, or at least let me know that I was going to be let down so badly, treated so badly, by Happy Haven bloody Hotels, wouldn't you?'

"I'm sure I can explain." I tried again, but in vain to complete a sentence.

"What is the point, I mean what is the point, the bloody point, I mean what is the point, the bloody real point, the real point of going to all the trouble to let you know that I am coming here tonight, and even you must agree that it is tonight only to find that I haven't got a room? Go on, tell me what is the point?"

"Well, Mr .... er... "

"And to make matters worse, you don't even know my name. Which proves, really proves, that you don't care whether I stay here or not. It is just a bloody joke to you that I haven't got a room for the night."

"I'm sure that I can arrange..."

"You couldn't arrange a piss-up in a brewery," he snarled.

He was seized by a violent spasm. He swayed sideways and almost tripped over his luggage. I reached out to steady him but he lurched forward unpredictably. Our heads met with a sickening crunch. Both of us swayed back up again. My eyes filled with tears and he just stood there holding his head.

"Damn you." he roared "damn and bloody blast you and all your lousy hotels." "stuff them," he yelled, "stuff them brick by brick and I hope it chokes you."

Ignoring his mixed metaphor, I said; "But I am sure-."

"You haven't heard the last of this. Oh no you haven't. Just you bloody wait. "You will be hearing more from my solicitors. My bloody solicitors will have you for breach of contract and assault. My solicitors will sue you for every penny you have. And when they have finished with you, you will have me to contend with. And I am really looking forward to that, oh yes, by the time I have finished with you won't know your arsehole from breakfast time."

"I'm sure I can explain. -" I said.

"Tell it to the judge" he said nastily.
He gathered his luggage and headed for the front door.

"Happy bloody Haven bloody Hotels are a bunch of poisoning bastards," he said.

In the light of our previous conversation it seemed like a new topic for discussion, but he had moved out of range. I straightened my jacket and tie. I gathered the few remaining shreds of my dignity and headed back to my office. Ethel and two junior receptionists were coping efficiently with many arrivals as I walked past the desk.

"I've always wanted to do that," she said without looking up.

"What?" I said.

"'Eadbutt an overbooking." she said, smiling.

"It was an accident," I said.
I could feel a bruise growing on my forehead and I hoped that the tears which were forming did not show. She gave me a broad and knowing wink.

The practice of overbooking guests in hotels is common. Although denied vehemently in public by Walter and all his competitors, it is normal. The unwritten rule states that overbooking of up to 30 percent of all rooms is O.K. in high demand areas. Hoteliers everywhere eagerly seek out high demand areas.

Such sites have a price beyond rubies. These are the sites where Walter builds his hotels and leaves his managers at the sharp end.

The punter who had been so rude to me had been a victim of this rule. He had telephoned on Monday and a provisional reservation was made. He was asked to confirm the booking in writing. In the event, his confirmation had not arrived, or had not been intercepted, in time. He was a provisional. There were 18 other provisionals that same day.

Crunch time for the punters who flock to Happy Haven Hotels is 6.p.m. By this critical time on Monday, Tuesday, Wednesday or Thursday evening you are at risk without a confirmed reservation. The Great Room Roulette wheel is set to spin by late afternoon. Winners and losers are declared immediately.

The vast majority of room reservations are booked and confirmed in advance and come to pass without a glitch. For the remainder, the first flutter of gaming begins when a casual guest wanders in during the late afternoon. A casual Enquirer starts the wheel turning;

"Have you got a room for to-night?"

This innocuous question posed in all innocence will ignite the blue touch paper. Well-trained receptionists strike the first note of terror.

"I'm very sorry," they say without a hint of compassion "but we are fully booked."

"Can you recommend another hotel?" is the next question.
"I'm afraid you won't get a room anywhere in the district, Sir, everywhere is fully booked."

It is just like a cold hand around your heart.

"Are you absolutely sure that you have nothing at all? Anything will do."

Some punters try charming smiles. This is as effective as bullets on King Kong. Others try bluster, which is equally ineffective. When the bluster or charm bit is over the real business begins.

"Well" say the receptionists; "we might just have something." By now fully in charge, like Nanny in the nursery. They are scanning the list of provisionals.

The receptionist is already ahead on points. She has removed any possibility of discussing a discount which the punter always wants if he/she believes that rooms are available.
She knows that unsold bed-space is a permanent loss by midnight. She knows that room sales generate other sales of food and booze at the undiscounted rate. She knows that "chance" guests are more willing to share rooms with total strangers if they can be made to believe that no alternative is available. She knows that she will earn a bonus for letting rooms, which are classified as vacant. She knows that provisional bookings may not arrive. Chance guests are those who do not have irrefutable proof of a reservation. This is a company document,

which arrives by snail mail, text or e-mail. It has a picture of Walter smiling happily in the top left corner. These company, or agency confirmations produce the daily rooming list. Any unreserved rooms are available for chance punters.

From 6 p.m. onwards, the provisionals are struck from the list. Their rooms are let to eager punters at the full rate. Single rooms command single rates. Two punters occupy twin beds. If demand is really high we set up beds in the ballroom and cots in the corridor. If a head hits a pillow, it is classified as a sleeper. At the end of the day, the magic ratios are produced for Head Office. Top of the list
is the average room rate per sleeper. The nearer you are to published tariff rates, the broader the smile at Head Office. You are getting into bonus territory now. Next in order of importance is the number of sleepers.
In my Happy Haven there are 140 twin-bedded rooms and 20 singles. I am looking for 300 sleepers every night. "Heads on pillows" ratios are about profits and Head Office get really excited about this.

Happy Haven managers all over the country watch their flocks of punters gathering every evening. Their motives are mixed. They are concerned to accommodate as many punters as possible because it is their job and because their salary is linked to profit.

Some managers show a most commendable pastoral care and touching regard for their charges. Other managers display a wholly cavalier disregard for the proprieties, or, even worse, discover within themselves the instincts of a flesh peddler.

Some, like me, are still trying to find a magic formula, which will persuade total strangers of the same species and gender to share rooms without rancour, animosity or chagrin (with the added incentive of a reasonably reduced tariff.)

"How many punters have we got tucked up tonight, Ethel?"
I ask the same question every evening. The nearer the answer is to three hundred, the happier I become. On one memorable occasion, the answer was three hundred and thirty, when a local tragedy attracted nearly one hundred news reporters and photographers to my patch for a brief, but memorable two days.
Ethel wears an enormous, bulbous pen around her slender neck. It dangles provocatively in the foothills of her boobs. She counts with it stuck firmly in her mouth.

"Two 'undred and free, Miss Tarnmond" she said, letting the pen slide back to a happier place. "And 11 no-shows so far."

No-shows are the bane of my life. Punters who book but do not arrive. They are the professional gamblers in the Room Roulette spin. They book without paying a deposit and may, or may not arrive.
I tried not to let anger, frustration and desperation set in. I did not succeed. My statistics for the day would not look good. Not enough heads on pillows. My masters at Head Office would not be pleased.

Like Salome, they like to see lots of heads on pillows.

CHAPTER 2 The Happy Pantry

By now, the Restaurant, -our Happy Pantry-was beginning to fill with early diners.

The diners who headed for the Pantry were to encounter a" meal experience". This is a ritual ordained by Walter, administered by acolytes in the Sanctuary Pantry, attested by minions in the Kitchen and served by wenches in striped surplices. Then it is all shovelled down with uncaring insensitivity by crass punters.

This ritual had been devised by Walter many years ago. Walter had been at the receiving end of a withering broadside fired by an acclaimed foodie. This damning indictment was published in a consumer guide with wide circulation.

The critic's wide but gullible readership had been entertained for many months afterwards by Walter's spirited defence. The locking of horns between an enraged privateer and a neutered critic had boosted circulation enormously. Both parties had derived considerable benefit from the exposure.

The foodie had suggested, quite accurately, that the food served in Walter's hotels was poor. That it was consistently bad in presentation, content and colour. And that it was served by hostile brigands.

An unfortunate experience in a Happy Haven had provoked the critic into near apoplexy. He had dwelt at some length on the convoluted skill that enabled steaks to be "tired". Soups to be "opaque".

Vegetables to be "flaccid". Salads to be "limp". Sweets to be "tacky". Beverages to be "thready". He had been most unhappy with his wine, too.
His observation that 'several wines of good provenance were inexpertly blended to produce a toxic cocktail misrepresented by a forger's label' was considered to be inflammatory by the pro-Walter lobby.

He described the waiters as anti-social thugs who were more suited to a career with the Mafia or Triad organisations.

Walter had reacted with customary vigour. He denied it all. He accused the critic of spiteful inaccuracy. He discovered something unsavoury in the critic's past and persuaded the tabloid press to disclose it. He attempted to sue the consumer guide that published the attack. When that failed he attempted to buy the guide. That also failed. But the critic had got the message. He pursued a less controversial career as an estate agent where his hyperbolic excess gave him a commercial edge over his competitors.

When the feathers had stopped flying, Walter recruited a band of catering advisors. Their brief was to improve the image of his Restaurants and increase their profit contribution to the group.
The advisors were to roam at will throughout the group. They set out to inspire the kitchen brigades with creative fervour. They listened patiently to all the long established excuses which prohibit any changes. They ignored all the excuses and found new chefs who were less obstructive.

They looked long and hard at the waiters. They were not impressed. They did not wish to be accused of racialism even if it was justifiable. They persuaded the French, Spanish, Italian, Portuguese and Philippino nationals that their best interests could be pursued elsewhere.

And in pursuit of that profit incentive, they replaced them all with women.

Under Walter's barbaric tutelage, this small band of hairy pink chefs and intense graduates invented the "Happy Pantry". Every Happy Haven has one. Thrice daily we lure our punters in to the Happy Pantry, not just to ingest a few thousand extra calories but also to have their taste buds tantalised, twisted and tormented by auto-suggestion and eye appeal.

"Our Happy Pantries" said the prophet Walter "shall be places where people want to go to be seen. And when they leave, they shall take fond memories with them and want to come back."

So they flock in, our epicurian lemmings. Their palates are dulled by pints of ale and fiery spirits. Their taste buds masked by nicotine. Their gastronomic appreciation honed to a fine edge by earlier encounters with unyielding bread-rolls and rocky Cornish Pasties. But their expectations are high.

They are welcomed in with gently smiling jaws. Ushered to a seat with a good view of all the other eager punters. They are fussed over with maternal

care. They are invited to have a drink before dining. They are given the wine-list. The menu is presented with a flourish. They are gently cross-examined to disclose their status. Room number or chance? Stayed here before? Any more in the party? Any special requests? Diets? Fads or fancies? Aversions? Ethnic or religious abstentions? Vegetarian or vegan?
Having screened out the critics, nuts and troublemakers we can get down to business.

"Would you like a starter?"
"What do you recommend?"
"We have; *Fresh sea-fruit Marie-Rose; Dew fresh cantaloupe schooners;*
"*Brine-soaked Bismark herring Capricorn; Layette of eggs Romanoff.*"

If the punter is confused by this list, it can be translated; Crab-sticks, melon, rollmops or hard boiled egg.
With luck, he will go for the one which sounds most familiar.

Whilst his selection is being delivered from the stack in the fridge, he can read on;

The main course choice is qualified by an extended footnote.

How about a steak? Good choice, that. *"Entrecote choisi du chef grille."*

Read on. It will be cooked to your choice somewhere on that confusing scale which begins with blue and ends with blasted. It will be impaled by a small gold pennant triumphantly endorsing your choice.

Be reassured that Walter's steaks are not just a slice from the end of a cryovac pac. They come from meadow grazed, home reared butch guys with cute forelocks and an alligator grin. Believe it, they gave themselves joyfully to the knackers yard just to excite your palate.

Cotelettes d agneau pre sale aux primeurs. That sounds good. Walter's lamb chops are special They do not arrive deep frozen in a container from New Zealand. They gambol happily through a truncated childhood in salt glazed meadows before springing with gay abandon to the slaughterers stunner. Their purpose is fulfilled on your plate. With "our logo" beaming at you happily from beneath a stack of straw potatoes, with the bleached ribs of Larry the Lamb crossed like soldiers swords at a wedding and dressed overall in vivid green watercress, who could fail to appreciate such a dish?

Not sold yet?

Then try our permutation of poultry.

From *Poussin, Poulet, Poularde, Coq and Volaille* take *Supreme, Cuisson, Aile, Filet or Tranche.* That is a chicken classified by age, gender and parts. Add any garnish from the list of 200 that starts with *Africaine* and ends with *Zingara.*

Prefix it with *Poche, Roti, Casserole, Grille, Frit or Saute* and you will never serve the same dish twice.

Or some fish? Walter's fish always smiles and wags his tail. He was a happy fish when he swam in the sea, river or fish farm. He has been on freezer hold for quite some time since those carefree days. But he will be born again on your plate, usually wearing a breadcrumb coat, a necklace of lemon and a buttonhole of parsley.

Then sample our vegetables. Not the flaccid ones of ill repute. An imposing list of products captured for your enchantment OUT OF SEASON. Be grateful to Captain Birdseye and his untiring band of cryogenic perverts. They can enmesh midsummers essence and hold it prisoner until the following summer, just for you.

Don't give in yet.

Look upon the sweet trolley. A confectioners sunset. A kaleidoscope of colour and contrast. A temptation of cream, chocolate, marzipan and puds. A feast of exotic fruits, alone or in concert. And an off-limits cache of *bombes, glaces, bavarois*. All smothered in cream.

Forget about the cholesterol scares. Don't worry about the waistline. A little more silt in the arteries wont do any real harm' will it?.

No? Go for the cheese trolley then.

Walter is there before you. His oafish smile peeps over the paper d' oyle. He is extolling the virtues of Cheddar, Leicester and Derby. He is winking at Brie, silver clad Camembert and naughty Danish

Blue. As tempting as a siren luring sailors to the Sea of Angina, killing you softly with surfeits.

Full up, then? Ready to give in? Must be time for coffee.

Walter's coffee is special. A precious, unique blend of rare beans. You have to try it to believe it.
We can fix it with any number of fiery spirits. With cream floating on top. Then it is Gaelic, Italic, Franctic or Manic coffee and you wont forget it. Have a cigar? Fat or thin, short or sharp? Even better, a custom built cigar" handrolled on the upper thigh of a dusky maiden in far off Caribee in one swift, suggestive movement.

A liqueur? A balloon of brandy? More coffee? Try a complimentary wafer, mint or *friandise*. Just a little something to prove that we care before we come to the bottom line.

'The *addition,* Sir? .' Of course. Just glance at it briefly over your distended middle. Sign it with a flourish. Charge it to your room? Or offer us your latest plastic smart card. You name it, we take it.

And remember your meal experience with Walter. Think of it as the apogee of your day. Treasure the memory of a fantasy which was almost a reality. The 'meal experience' is almost finished, just one more ritual to indulge.
'Good night, Sir or Madame,' we chant with Walter's approval. "have a Good Night.'

CHAPTER 3 STRIP POKER

When you negotiate your job with Happy Haven Hotels (the only time when you have a bargaining edge) the final option is;

"Do you want to live in or out?".

Older hands immediately counter; "What difference does it make to the pay?"

Then the bargaining begins again.

In my eagerness to be a Happy Haven manager I said "Yes" to living-in. It was my first management appointment and I was keen to make a good impression on my interviewer.

I discovered after the first month that my pay had been docked by a fifth to cover the cost of living-in.

Living-in means that you eat drink and sleep in the hotel. Living-out means that you eat and drink in the hotel, but sleep somewhere else.

The advantages of living-out raced through my mind when I answered the telephone in the early hours.

"Night Manager, Mr Hammond".
The voice sounded loud and cheerful.
"Well?"
"There's a disturbance on the fourth floor".
"What's it all about?".

"Some of the gentlemen have had too much to drink and the young lady isn't having it".
"Come again?"
"Some of the gentlemen are a little worse for wear and the young lady is shouting very loud."
"What is she shouting about?"
"Well, you see, sir, some of the gentlemen have had too much to drink and............ "
"Yes, I know that. What is she shouting about?"
"You mean the young lady, sir?"
"Of course I mean the young lady."
"Oh yes, the young lady."
"Well?"
"Well what, sir?"
"What is she shouting about?" By now I am shouting too. There was a long pause.
"I wonldn't want to repeat what she said, sir."
He sounded a bit miffed.
"Why not?"
"Well, sir" he said finally, "its rude.".

Now if there is one blessing that can be granted to a hotel manager, it is a night Manager in full possession of his marbles.

I am so blessed. My night Manager is a stalwart. A man of immense capability and excellent judgement. I can rely upon him to cope with everything whilst I sleep.
Walter's multi-million asset and his sleepers are safe in Mr Travers capable and reliable hands.
But even Mr Travers must have his two nights off every week.

He is relieved by an inchoate oaf named Harry. It was Harry who had just informed me that there was a disturbance on the fourth floor.

My night gear was ready. Cords and a training sweater. Cowboy boots, a Night Stick and a broad leather belt. The gear for all occasions from a fire drill to a punch-up.

This looked like a punch-up. I slipped the squat leather truncheon down my cords. I cursed when the smooth leather slid cold across my belly.

I thought briefly of my two Trainee Assistant Managers. Two ardent youths recently graduated from college. They are entrusted to my care for further, practical education in hotel management.

Both are soft faced, beardless youths with pimples. They are known affectionately as Pinky and Perky. They do not live-in. It is not considered wise to expose the very young to the seamier side of hotel management.

Even if either were in the hotel, I doubt if they could have helped. Drunks respond far better to curses and imprecations than to timid requests. Both Pinky and Perky tend to pipe a little when pressed. I have a fairly well rounded range of obscenities and threats which I learned from Chefs to fall back on, so I went out like the Lone Ranger.

The journey to the fourth floor seemed interminable.
Passenger lifts seem to go slower in emergencies as if they are holding out for fewer passengers or

higher voltage. An infection that lifts catch from the doleful engineers who service them.

Harry was waiting for me in the foyer of the fourth floor.

"Its still going on." he said. He nodded several times, pleased about something.

The corridors of all hotels are divided into short sections by smoke doors. The smoke doors are designed to make departure easy and arrival difficult. The smoke doors snap at you when you arrive like angry alligators. You must be adroit to get through in one piece. If you are carrying luggage, they get you every time, just like the Canadian Mounties.

Bitter experience has taught me that you must never approach a disturbance cautiously. If you stand there and cough apologetically everyone ignores you. The more dramatic the arrival, the more likely you are to have the upper hand.

So when I burst through the last set of smoke doors and said;

"What the hell is going on here?" I had the undivided attention of four guests.

Three of the guests were men in various states of undress. The fourth was a girl. She was fully dressed. She smiled at me, amused.

"Absolutely nothing at all" said a tall young man wearing a shirt and floral underwear, "absolutely nothing at all."

"She started it." said another, clad in thunder and lightning dressing gown and fluorescent socks.

"What the hell has it got to do with you?" said the small pink one with a shiny bald head and droopy moustache. He was overdressed by comparison with the others. He was wearing platform soles and swayed hypnotically as he spoke.

"Screw the lot of you" said the girl.
In a factual, friendly way, like the introduction to the news.

"Which rooms are you in?" I asked no-one in particular.
"That one", said droopy moustache aggressively, "and what the hell has it got to do with you?"

"Four-one-one." said thunder and lightning, like the bright one in class.

"I really am most dreadfully sorry," said the lanky one.

"Bastards, all of you." said the girl with a friendly smile.

"I am the manager here." I said to keep the discussion group going.

"In that case," said droopy moustache, "I want to complain about the service."

"I've never been in trouble in my life before" said lanky. "I really am most dreadfully sorry."

"It's all her fault" said thunder and lightning, "she led us on."

"Sweetheart" said the girl, "that just ain't true. You are a lying sonovabitch."

"Oh golly." said lanky.
"That's a bit strong." said thunder and lightning.
"Exactly what I mean," said droopy, turning to me. "What are you going to do about his sort of thing? After all, you are the manager here" if he had been wearing more clothes, he might have sounded dignified.

The girl was looking at me, smiling brightly without wavering.

"Gentlemen," I said sternly, "the best thing by far is that you all return to your rooms at once.
" Oh golly," said lanky, "I really am most dreadfully sorry."

He seemed to be the weakest of the group. I concentrated on him. "What are you sorry about" I asked, "the disturbance you are creating in my hotel, or going back to your room?"

Lanky started convulsively and began to stutter incomprehensibly.

"That is not the right way to talk to a guest."
Droopy moustache again.
I could see that he was going to be a problem.

"I can't go back." said lanky, in a moment of relative lucidity.

"Why not?" I tried to sound menacing.

"I've locked myself out."

"Stupid bastard." said the girl.

"Harry" I called loudly, "Harry, come here."
"Yes, Mr Hammond" said Harry. "I am here."
Meaning the other side of the smoke door.

"Take this guest back to his room and let him in"

"You." I said sharply to lanky, "go with the night Manager and he will let you into your room."

"What room would that be?" asked Harry.
"I don't know." I snarled, "ask him."
"I'm not really sure" said lanky, "I really am most dreadfully sorry."
"He doesn't know which room he is in ." said Harry to me.
"Jesus Christ." said the girl.

"Harry", I said slowly and clearly. "take him to reception and check him against the rooming list. His name will be on the rooming list.
You do know your name?" I directed the question to lanky who had become incoherent again.

"Very well, Mr Hammond. " said Harry. He led lanky away, chatting happily. That left me with four-one-one, thunder and lightning and droopy, from over there. Plus the girl, who was still smiling.

"Where" I said to Droopy, "are the rest of your clothes?" He swayed upright, like a round bottom doll.

"Now see here." he began. He had difficulty in staying upright. He did not finish the sentence.

"Damned impertinence." he said.

He swayed off to a nearby room with an open door. "Never been so insulted in all my life." he said. The door slammed shut and I heard the tinkle of breaking glass.

That left four-one-one. Thunder and lightning. I gave him my undivided attention.

"Just a cotton-pickin' moment" said the girl, "this one is mine." She advanced towards him. Thunder and lightning cringed.
"Now lets not be unreasonable" he said" just remember a short while ago we were all good friends."
He backed slowly towards the nearest smoke doors, his arms held up in surrender. "Just remember the good times, Baby". She followed him, step by slow step.

"Listen, sweetie," he said. "Do you remember when we were all in there playing poker?"
"Yeah," she said, "I remember."
"Well, " he said, "it was fun, wasn't it?"
He sounded strained. A few octaves too high.
"No it wasn't." she said evenly.

"But" he said. "It was marvellous at the time. We were all having such good fun."

"Buster," she said. "You was having all the fun. I was bored." She raised her hands slowly, shoulder high. Thunder and lightning looked petrified.

She pushed him with both hands and he swayed back against the smoke door. Very neatly, she kneed him in the balls. The pain showed in his eyes and he sucked in a great draught of air. He leaned forward in obeisance. He cupped his groin in his hands and moaned softly. Then he swayed off to the sanctuary of four-one-one, blissfully close at hand.

The girl dusted her hands noisily.

"He was a sore loser." she said.

As an explanation, it seemed inadequate. I did not say so, but I thought the punishment was much too severe for the crime. I had taken a deep breath as a reflex action when thunder and lightning was struck. My knees were tight together as the girl walked towards me.

"You were playing poker with them? What kind of poker?".

"Strip." she said. "to jailhouse rules."

"Then how come you still have all your clothes on? None of the men did."

She looked at me and grinned mischievously.

"I'm real good at poker. My Daddy taught me all the rules when I was five."

"Are you a professional gambler?" I had a vested interest in the answer.

"Hell, no." she laughed.

"I'm the trail guide with Transition Tours.
"I have a coach party for Troon and Fort William, Scotland. We are staying here and leave early tomorrow morning."

I remembered them. A party of 44 tourists booked in from Head Office. I was about to suggest that she should return to her room when she said, pointing to my groin;

"Is that for real?" She emphasised "real".

I followed her gaze downwards. The leather truncheon had slipped inside my cords, raising a path from groin to belt. I put my hand down and raised the truncheon to rest comfortably behind the belt.

"Jee-sus." she said.

"All part of the management service." I said.
The girl advanced towards me. I braced instinctively.

"Hi," she said, "my name is Naomi. Naomi Dwight" .... she made it sound like one long word ....

34

"from Nantucket, Nantucket Island, Noo England, U.S. of A"

I moved cautiously within range of that formidable right knee.

I decided to be equally frank but more pithy.

"Martin Hammond. Manager here."

I shook her hand warily.

"Do you think we could get a cup of coffee somewhere?". she asked.

I relaxed a little. Suddenly she seemed to be less formidable.

"Yes, of course." I said.

I followed Naomi-Naomi Dwight along the corridor to the lift. I was curious to find out why she had been playing strip poker with 3 other guests in the small hours when she was due to depart early in the morning.

It was also a mystery why an attractive young woman should be part of an unseemly squabble on the fourth floor. Some questions needed an answer, if only to satisfy my curiosity. I would use her response to broaden my experience of management and women at the same time.

My glance strayed to this outspoken and forceful guest.

She was both slender and sensuous, trim and lithe with a slightly athletic, bouncy walk. She wore a straight, dark skirt with deep pleats which did nothing to impede her rapid stride and free movement, as another guest had so recently discovered. Above the skirt, she wore a white blouse, primly collared and cuffed like an airline hostess. Under close-cropped, fair hair, layered like feathers, her neck was long and slender. I could see smooth, unruffled skin moving sinuously over her vertebrae as I followed close behind her.

Facing her in the lift, she passed another appraisal with flying colours. She was just as attractive from the front as she was from the rear.

In my experience, not many women pass that test. I have suffered many a grievous disappointment whilst idly watching female guests in the lobbies of many hotels. Watching female guests is one of the more agreeable fringe benefits that hotel managers enjoy although not many ladies pass the fore-and aft test.

The retreating female form can be most deceiving. It is the lack of erogenous zones which make the rear view so tantalising. There is so little communication from astern. It is all beamed forward. Just a shape, a form, a wiggle and a waft of perfume are all that you get to go on. From these signals, I build up my own impression of the flip side.

I have indulged many day dreams this way. I have also known many fantasies turn to ashes this way.

Naomi-Naomi Dwight from Nantucket, Nantucket Island, Noo England, U.S. of A. registered very high on my scale of approval. She looked good from all angles, like a precious, illustrated vase. I took her to the Coffee Shop and brewed some fresh coffee.

An hour and several coffees later, we were still in the Coffee Shop. Naomi said;

"Martin, you just gotta believe me."

"What I have to believe," I said, trying not to sound negative, "is that you booked in here with your tour group, went to the bar for a drink, got picked up by one of my guests, had Dinner with another guest, and ended up in yet another guest's room playing strip poker with two more.?"

"That's not the way it was."

"Why did you do it?" I was surprised by my own question. It was really none of my business and I shouldn't have cared about the answer. But in our short acquaintance this unusual and very attractive punter had got to me.

She shrugged expansively.

"It seemed like a good idea at the time." she said.

"Christ Almighty", I said strongly, "you have only been in my hotel for a few hours and you have involved a dozen or so of my guests in your shennanagins already."

She had this disconcerting habit of smiling at me whenever I spoke.

"If you were to stay here for any length of time" I said, "the whole hotel would just seize up. It would be anarchy."

Her smile did not fade when she said;

"That just ain't so."

"Well." I said, "you will just have to let me be the judge of that. Believe me when I
tell you that the hotel would come to a standstill. It would be a disaster if all my guests just ran around all night playing games in each other's bedrooms."

"No, no," she said, "not that."

"Not what?"

"Not the bit about the anarchy. You are right about that. You couldn't have people running around all night."

I must have looked puzzled. She said

"I had dinner with Timothy."

"So?"

"Well. Timothy was playing poker upstairs."

"What the hell has that got to do with anything?"

The smile went down a little and the eyebrows went up to compensate.

"You said that the guy who bought dinner wasn't the guy who played poker."

"Did I say that?"

"Yeah," she said, "and he was."

"Alright," I said, "I was wrong about one small detail. What were you doing playing strip poker in the first place?"

"I was killing time with the guys."

"Do you do that often? I mean, do you play a lot of poker?".

"Some."she said, "back home we often play poker."

"But with complete strangers? Isn't that risky?"

"Timothy isn't a stranger." she said.

"He isn't?"

"Nope", She shook her head several times.

"Then who is he?"

"He works with me at Transition Tours."

"What does he do?"

I tried to remember Timothy. He must have been the
incoherent one who apologised a lot.

"He drives the coach".

"And plays strip poker?"

"Yep," she said, " he isn't very good at it yet. But he's learning."

"Why didn't you tell me that earlier. It does make a difference, you know."

"What difference does it make?"

"If you were known to the others, it puts you in a different light."

"It does?"

"Oh yes," I said "that's a totally different kettle of fish."

There was a long pause. Naomi looked at me without wavering.

"Have I got it right? It's O.K. to play poker with people you know, but's it's not O.K. to play poker with people you don't know? What the hell is that? House rules.?"

"Something like that" There was another long pause.

"You Brits are crazy bastards." she said it without rancour.

"Just tell me one more thing. What was all that squabble in the corridor about?"

"They were sore losers. It was getting late and I wanted to go home. They wanted to play some more.

The janitor came along and must'a thought we were fighting. We weren't. "

She was smiling again. A broad, believable smile. I believed her because I wanted to believe in her .

"I think there has been a misunderstanding here" I said. "Will you excuse me for disturbing so much of your night?"

"You want me to excuse you?" She shook her head.

"I will never understand you Brits. You say the craziest things."

"Well, old girl," I said, being obligingly British,

"Shall I walk you back to your room, dontchaknow?"

"Crazy bastards" she said, shaking her head slowly.

I walked her back to her room and opened it with my master swipe.

"Good night, Naomi-Naomi Dwight" I said, "sleep well in what is left of it."

I leaned forward in imitation of a teutonic bow to kiss her. I still had not forgotten that formidable right knee. Very adroitly, she deflected the kiss to her right cheek.

"Goodnight." She said it softly with eyes averted. Then she was gone.

I saw Naomi three hours later in the reception foyer. She looked bright-eyed and bushy tailed as she shepherded her group of tourists onto the coach, bound for Fort William and Troon, Scotland.

We were both very busy but we managed to meet for a brief moment.

"Come back again soon, Naomi-Naomi Dwight. "

"You betcha ass" she replied.

CHAPTER 4 PINKY AND PERKY

I am never at my best in the morning. Some people are. I am not one of them. It is all a matter of metabolic rates, I am told. In which case my meta-balls are at their best from mid-day onwards.

So by applying inverse ratio Sod's Law, which states that maximum hassle will always coincide with minimum resources, my busiest time will always be in the morning.

Pinky and Perky, my assistant managers, arrive at the hotel early every morning. They are refreshed by deep, undisturbed sleep. They are buoyed up by their juvenile enthusiasm and sober good habits.

They radiate Boy Scout virtues, clean living and student thrift. They are eager to please, swift to serve and programmed to be really useful. I used to be like that. Seven years ago that description would have fitted me. At the tender age of 27, I too, can sigh for my lost youth.

Pinky and Perky are ardent collectors of problems. Every day they visit all the hotel's operating departments and confer with the staff there to discover any new or potential problems which will be discussed at the daily management meeting.

"Iceberg" said Pinky -he means the head housekeeper-" says that 407 is a mess. Broken glass on the floor, wardrobe door off, torn shower curtain and blood all over the carpet and bathroom floor."

He read from his notes "and a pack of playing cards on the bed?" He sounded puzzled.

"It can happen." I said, "after a game of poker."

"I beg your pardon?"

"Particularly if you are a sore loser and accidentally tread on a broken glass without being aware of it."

"I beg your pardon?"

"Never mind," I said. "charge him one hundred and twenty-five quid for the damage and stick it on his bill."

"One hundred and twenty-five?" said Pinky.

"That's right" I said, "One hundred and twenty-five."

In a way I was glad that it was Droopy. Serve the bastard right.

"Take 407 off the status sheet until it is re-decorated." I said.

Pinky scribbled something busily in his note book
.
"She also said that we really must do something about the linen-hire firm."

"She always says that."

Pinky consulted his notebook. "She was short 28 pillow cases, 34 sheets, 17 towels and 2 sets of chefs whites." he announced.

Make sure that she gets a credit note from linen hire"

Pinky was writing busily again.

"Tiles have come off the wall in 371, 379, 405, 421, 493, 504, 532 .... "

"Send a note to maintenance. Tell them to get their fingers out."

"Fingers out" muttered Pinky, still writing.

"25 light bulbs are needed, in rooms 384, 376, 401, ... "

"Tell maintenance about that too."

"Corridor lighting on the third, outside 320 and on the fifth by 513 has failed and emergency lighting on the second .... "

"Tell maintenance to do the emergency lights first, then the others."

"The net curtains on the third floor are all coming down today to be washed. They won't be replaced until to-morrow,"

"Tell reception. They can put all the flashers on the third floor and they can have themselves a ball."

"I beg your pardon?"

Pinky takes his job very seriously.

"Just tell reception about the net curtains."
"Iceberg says that the room-maids are becoming more and more narked about serving early morning teas.

They want extra money for it."
"If you mention money, I go deaf and blind." I said Incredibly, Pinky wrote something down in his notebook.

"She is short of soap-tablets, tea-spoons and Walter brochures."

"Issue some more from stock."

"She also says that the rooming list was wrong last night. Five were shown as stopovers and didn't stay."

"Jesus Christ" I said without rancour. "I could have taken five more sleepers last night. The overbookings gave me a seriously bad time too."

Pinky looked alarmed. He scribbled busily in his note-book.

"Find out," I said, "which bloody idiot produced that rooming list. And find out whether or not we can charge a cancellation fee .. And find out whether they paid or not.If it is a company account, we can stuff them on the bill anyway."

One of the mechanisms open to hotel managers is to add charges to company bills and hope that they will be met by default. By the time the account is paid, the details are often forgotten. Overpayment is common and profits are augmented this way, effectively cancelling some of the discount due to large corporate clients.

"Ethel says she is one receptionist short this evening and we have 28 overbooked."

"We will deal with that lot when the time comes. In the meanwhile, it will make a major contribution to to my continuing sanity if we can get the bloody rooming list right in the first place."

I banged my clenched fist down hard on the desk. Several items jumped into the air and landed with a crash. I regretted doing it. It made my headache worsen.

"What about the the one short in reception?" Pinky looked petrified.

"Mr Postlethwaite." I said. That is Pinky's real name.

"What are you doing this evening?"

"It is my half-day.! am going to the Horse of the Year Show" he said smugly.

"Oh no you're not."

"I'm not?"

"Nope, " I said, "you are duty receptionists instead."

Perky doesn't use a note-book. He carries a clip board with a large crocodile jaw at the top. Perky is a hairpin of a man. His rapidity of movement is completely cancelled out by his slowness of speech. He doesn't actually stutter but the words don't come out very fast.

Perky's area of interest is Food and Beverage. Whilst Pinky is talking to the Housekeeper, Receptionists, Maintenance and Porters, Perky is talking to the Chef, Restaurant Manager, Bars Manager, Banquetting Manager and Comptroller.

"How many diners last night?" I asked.

"Seventy-two."

I scowled. Seventy-two diners from two hundred and thirty sleepers was bad news. It meant that another nasty ratio would appear on my Head Office returns.

"How much did we take in the bars last night?"

"Seven hundred and seventy-four pounds and sixty-three pence."

That was better. In my Happy Haven I have a dedicated team of boozers. They take their task seriously. Which is more than can be said for the diners.

Perky has an enormous Adam's Apple. It bobs up and down before he speaks.

"The staff are complaining about the food in the Staff Canteen."

"All staff, everywhere, complain about the food in Staff Canteens. What is new about that?"

"It is different this time," he said. "The complaint is that the food for the staff is fattening. Some are overweight."

I completed a mental roll-call of the 80 staff in my Happy Haven. Not many of them were overweight. Chef and the Restaurant Manager were a bit corpulent, but the majority of us were fairly slender and fit. Not many outsize uniforms here.

"Tell chef to offer everyone a choice of salads instead of cooked meals. That should sort the fat cats ."

"When should this start?"

"How about to-day". Perky wrote something at great length on his clip-board.

"Has the bar stock report come in yet?" I asked. Perky shook his head. "Not yet."

That meant that the monthly inquisition of the Bars Manager would be delayed a little longer.

Every month, after the stock report had been compiled by independent assessors, the summary was sent to me. Every month the figures showed that whilst irrefutable proof of dishonesty was not available, some doubt lingered in their minds about absolute integrity.

But every month the Bars Manager introduced some new shreds of information and convinced me that the assessors were mistaken in their belief.

He was given the benefit of the doubt. I looked eagerly for the usual signs that betray the dishonest. There was no evidence of conspicuous consumption or any of the other hall-mark. He had an old motor-car.,His suits were shabby. He did not sport the latest electronic goodies .He did not go away on expensive foreign holidays. The Scottish verdict would be "Not proven."

"What about the Food Report?"

Perky nodded vigorously.

"It is nearly ready."

My weekly Food Report was yet another piece of consistent bad news. It was compiled in-house by my comptroller, a swarthy Pakistani gentleman. It revealed all food costs as a ratio of all food sales. After making an allowance for the cost of feeding the staff, it was supposed to leave a profit margin of 65%. Mine had always hovered depressingly in the lower fifties. On one horrendous occasion it had struck the upper forties. It would be a grain of comfort if the upper fifties had been achieved.

"What have we on the Functions list to-day?"

"A seminar for 35. The Young Lions lunch for 55. Two interview rooms. And a wedding Reception for 90."

"That sounds quite good. Any problems there?"

"I am afraid so." Perky said after a double swallow." You see, the chef didn't know about the wedding until yesterday."

"Why is that a problem?" I asked, "the menu isn't tricky, is it?"

"It is not the menu which has caused the problem."

"Well, what then? We are not double booked, are we?"

"No, not double booked" said Perky deliberately. He gathered himself visibly.

"We forgot to order the cake."

His words came at me like an Exocet missile. Homing in for the kill.

"Which bloody idiot took the bloody booking."

Blood was rushing around my system, trying to bust out of the veins. I did not bang the desk again as that was more painful than therapeutic. But I did see a red mist swirling around my head.
.
Perky swallowed noisily three times. He handed me a sheet of paper from his clip board. It was a standard Function Booking form which contained

all the details of the event. It was all written down there. Details from time of wedding ceremony right through to time of departure with all the featured highlights in between.

It was completed in my own handwriting. I had also dictated and sent a letter of confirmation which assured the bride's mother that the cake would have three tiers and a statuette of a bride and groom on top. I could even recall the bride's mother from our meetings and telephone calls.

A formidable woman of great girth with the presence and bearing of a battleship. Pinky chose that moment to put his head round the door.

"About that rooming list"

"Well?"

"It was produced by Janet. She is the one that is off sick."

"Just make sure that Ethel does the rooming list today. I have got another problem to see to."

I was still thinking about where to get a three tier wedding cake with a statuette of a bride and groom on top when Ethel appeared at the door.

"Miss Tammond" she said "there's a punter out 'ere who won't pay his bill. Says it's too much."

"Which room is he in?"

"407."

It was that bastard Droopy back again.

"Tell him" I said slowly "that considering the damage he has caused, it is cheap at the price."

"Hullo, hullo," I said into the telephone.

Perky had dialled the confectioners who make wedding cakes for us.

"You don't happen to have a three tier wedding cake with a bride and groom on top that says Congratulations to Bernard and Stephanie, do you?"

"Just one moment" said a remote voice, "I'll put you through to the bakery."

"Miss Tammond". Ethel had returned.

"What is it now?"

"That bloke says it wasn't him that caused the damage. It was someone else."

"Tell him to get stuffed."

"Yes, Miss Tammond."

"What was that you said?" It was a voice from the phone.

"No, no, not you." I said "I wasn't talking to you."

"Are you all right?" said the voice.

53

"Yes, of course I am." I said " I just rang you up to see if you happen to have a three tier wedding cake with a bride and groom on top and Congratulations to Bernard and Stephanie on the top layer.

"What colour?"

"White" I said, "with blue piping."

"Round or square?"

"Square," I said, "with a silver base."

"Take about three weeks." he said.

"Miss Tammond."

"What?"

"That bloke from 407."

"Well?"

"He's going to complain to 'ead office."

"You don't understand," I said into the phone "I must have it to-day."

And to Ethel. "Tell him I will be with him in a moment."

"I could rush it through and do it for you in two weeks" said the voice helpfully.

"No, no," I said desperately, "I must have it now."

54

"I don't think it can be done" said the voice. "It is not long enough." He sounded a bit pained.

"There's a lot of work goes into a three tier cake, you know, you can't just throw them together.

"Ethel!" I roared. No reply ....

"and it takes hours and hours of piping with several nozzles .... "

"Ethel!"

"Yes, Miss Tammond?"

"Where's 407?"

"Gorn" she said. "Left his address so you can write to him." ....

"of course we will need to know what sort of pillars to use for the supports and then I can give you a quotation.

"Can you do it to-day? Yes or no."

"No."

"Then get off the bloody line."

The phone rang the moment that I put it down.

"Miss Tammond"

"Yes."

"'ead office on the line for you."

"Jesus Christ," I said, "that was quick."

The caller from Head Office was a charming young woman from Group Purchasing. She wanted to know if I was happy with the latest delivery of book matches featuring Walter on the front cover. I was able to give her the reassurance she sought without diluting the most immediate matter.

Perky said;

"There is a cake shop in the shopping mall which always has a wedding cake in the window."

"Ring them and see if they have a three tier, square cake with 'Congratulations to Bernard and Stephanie' on top."

I dialled the chef in his kitchen.

"Chef," I said,"we have a problem."

"The wedding cake," he said "No?"

"The wedding cake. Yes." I said. "we haven't got one."

Present my chef with a problem and you unleash a non-stop stream of his native dialect, mostly mid European gutteral. The stream is best left to run it's own course.

I put the phone on the desk and said to Perky; "Any luck?" His adam's apple rose and fell thrice.

"Keep trying."

Chef was still flowing well. I left him to it.

Pinky returned to the office.

"Well?"

"We haven't got enough tea-spoons."

"Mr Bouverie-Adams." I said his name very slowly and deliberately. "Piss off."

Chef was down to *andante con moto* by now. I said;

"What about the cake?"

I listened very carefully to what he had to say. That is the only way to understand what he means. Two words in every ten are very significant. But you never know which two. So I listen and sort at the same time.

"I suppose it will work if all else fails. We must be prepared to try it."

"Thank you, chef," I said, "I will see you later".

"Mr Postlethwaite," I said, "this is what we are going to do about the missing cake." He swallowed six times on the trot. He said; "It will never work." "Have faith." I said "it can move mountains." My phone rang. "Miss Tammond? ' ead Office for you."

My adrenalin was circulating well today. I braced myself ready for the onslaught. "Mr Gammon?" said a plum in mouth voice.

"My name is Hammond"

"Doesn't look like it from up here. Your writing is not very clear."

"Who are you?"

"Head Office Control" he said.

"Oh, the Kremlin," I said "you are checking up on your KGB agents."

"Don't be facetious. I was just getting your name right, that's all." He sounded a bit miffed.

"What do want me for? Alleged breach of standing orders? Failure to execute plans on time? Insufficient dedication to quotas and targets?"

"I haven't received your Weekly Report yet."

"That's because I haven't sent it yet."

"This isn't the first time you've been late. It makes like really difficult for us chaps up here when you don't get your reports out on time."

The sort of complaint that Generals used to make about infantry in the trenches.

"We do have other things to do. Like making the profit so that you can count it."

"I shall expect to receive it tomorrow." he snapped.

"Up yours!" I said. When the receiver was safely back on it's cradle.

I dialled the control office in the hotel.

"Ibrahim," I said, "is the Weekly Report completed yet?" Ibrahim is a portly, grave looking Pakistani gentleman. He wears Western suits and a turban.

He looks and sounds like the genie from Alladin's cave.

"It is very nearly so."

"How does it look?"

"It is not a pretty picture. It does not make very important reading."

"Fill in all the figures in pencil. Then bring it up to me for a shuftee."

"It shall be done as you wish." He sounded unhappy.

After that there was a pause. An unusual quiet descended on my office. It was like being in the eye of a hurricane. I was waiting for the other half of the storm to build up.

I ordered some coffee. I looked at the morning mail to see if any other problems were creeping up on me. The surface signs were all calm and the hotel looked orderly and neat. But I could sense a far off disturbance gathering pace as it closed in like an avenging angel.

CHAPTER 5 THE WEDDING PARTY

Twenty five letters and one rigged Weekly Report later I was informed that the bride's mother had arrived. Perky did not have to tell me that it was Mrs Courtenay. He just said; "She's here."

The Robinson-Courtenay Wedding Reception was to be held in the Blue Suite. The Blue Suite has it's own entrance from the car park and a private lobby.

The bride and groom and their respective parents can stand in line to receive their guests in the lobby.

Then they can pass through to the Blue Suite where the Wedding Breakfast will be served.

Nine circular tables were laid to take ten guests each. The Top Table was a straight which would seat the principals, 14 in all, including bride and groom, their parents, best man and bridesmaids.

We always decorate the Top Table to a higher standard than the rest. Walter says so. The front is garlanded by the florists, heavy candelabra are strategically placed amongst the flower troughs, tall stemmed green hock glasses glow and we even let them have real linen serviettes. The guests have to make do with paper ones.

The Top Table is the focal point of the function and the room lighting scheme sets it into sharp focus.

Resplendent in the bull's eye of this display was a Wedding Cake on a gleaming silver plinth.

A round one, to be sure, and only two tiers, with a message on top. But a Wedding Cake nonetheless

Mrs Courtenay had not diminished in size or presence since our last meeting. The pre-nuptial organisation which usually runs the bride's mother ragged had just bounced of her armour, leaving her confidence undented and her nerve ends unsplit.

"Mr Hammond" she said with unsmiling eyes, "how good of you to meet me."

I put on my best smile. Years of bitter experience have taught me to spit in the bleary eye of disaster once it is close enough.

"Did the ceremony go well at St Michaels?" I had re-read my notes on the booking form very thoroughly since this morning.

"Reasonably well" she said "but the choir was undisciplined."

Perky hovered close at hand and said "May I take your coat, Madame?"

When she handed her coat to him, her dress rustled and hissed like a rapier being drawn from its scabbard.

"Can I show you the arrangements before your guests arrive, Mrs Courtenay?"

She had arrived ahead of the pack by bullying the photographers into changing their schedule. The rest of her family were still posing for pictures outside the church. "Please do" she said, following.

I lingered as long as possible over the trivia, like the type of sherry to be served, the reception line-up, guest's loos, the seating plan. I even managed to steer her to the room put at the bride's disposal for changing into her departure dress.

Finally, she said;"I would like to see the meal arrangements, Mr Hammond."

"But of course," I said, back teeth on display.

By sheer good fortune, Mrs Courtenay started by inspecting the round guest's tables. She found a glass with a thumb print on it. I managed to turn this into a finger-snapping, tut-tutting session with the waiting staff who were on stand-by.

Then she discovered from the guest tent cards that Uncle Jack was seated at the same table as Auntie Francis. It took some more precious moments to discover that it was impossible to move Uncle Jack to another table as he was liable to generate even more offence elsewhere.

"I will now look at the Top Table," she announced with a rustle, a hiss and a snap.

I followed meekly.

Some of the knives and forks lacked the millimetric precision of place that the occasion demanded. She re-arranged them deftly. One or two flowers were twitched a little and a chair re-positioned before she focused her attention on the cake.

She stiffened like a soldier on parade. She turned on me with an agility that her age and size belied.

"Mr Hammond!" she said "what is the meaning of this?"

"The cake, you mean?" I did not recognise my own voice.

"Of course I mean the cake!"

"I am going to explain about the cake."

"Well get on with it then."

"In the early hours of this morning, " -I had rehearsed this speech earlier-"the confectioners were putting the finishing touches to your cake.

Three tiers, iced in white and piped in blue with Congratulations to Bernard and Stephanie on top and a statuette of a bride and groom ....
"Get to the point" ....
"He loaded the cake into his van and set out for the hotel. He comes here quite often, you know? "

I had hoped that the personal touch would be well received. I was mistaken. Her glare intensified and she said; "Get on with it, Man."

"He was at the junction of High Street and Market Street when he was involved in an unfortunate accident."

"What happened?" she said it through clenched teeth.

"The van turned over"
"What happened to the cake?"
"It turned over, too."
"Where is the cake now?"
I was not expecting that. It was not in my script. "In the kitchen." I said it too quickly.
"What happened to the driver?"
I wasn't expecting that either.
"He's all right. Shaken and stirred, but all right."
That was another mistake. I could feel her temperature rising.

"My first reaction, Mrs Courtenay, on hearing the sad news, was to telephone you at home and ask you to cancel the wedding .... " The temperature went up a couple more degrees, so I said hastily, " ..... but that was obviously not on...... . She relaxed a little.
" ..... so I called my management team together to see what to do for the best on the most important day in your daughter's life .... "

"That cake" she said, pointing, "whose is it?"

"Tomorrow," I said, "the Blue Suite is being used for another function ..... "

"Whose cake is that?" she snarled

"It was made for this couple who are coming here to celebrate their Diamond Jubilee."

"Then, Mr Hammond"-she sounded like a judge passing sentence-"that would be why it says Congratulations to Bert and Millie on your 50th Anniversary on top?"

I just nodded. "How dare you. How dare you. How dare you." she said on a rising crescendo.

"It seemed like a good idea at the time." I offered.

One of those pregnant pauses followed. Eventually, I said; "Mrs Courtenay, please? There is another little matter I must mention."

"You will pay for this." She said it twice, nodding her head vigorously.

"Mrs Courtenay, please listen to me for a moment?"

She focused twin laser beams on me.

"Well?" she hissed.

"Do you think, Mrs Courtenay" I gulped "that you could ask your daughter not to cut the cake?"

She took one step towards me and I said hurriedly "...... we need it again to-morrow, you see."

She came even closer.

" .... .I have talked to the photographer and he can take a picture of your daughter just holding the

66

knife and pretending to cut the cake -if we turn the cake round, the bit that says "Congratulation to" will show but" Bert and Millie" will be hidden........."I trailed off.

She was gathering herself for a statement, so I said.

"After all, when the cake is cut up into little pieces and put into little white boxes nobody will know where it came from, will they? We might even be able to use the bits from the broken one." I said, trying to be helpful.

"How about letting us put the bits of cake into little white boxes for you?"

"You are an incompetent, stupid fool." she said "you will rue this day's work and you will pay for it dearly. What you have done will be punished severely and you will pay for it dearly. You are incompetent, stupid and foolish."

She was beginning to sound like an overbooking so I settled down into my being dumped on mode.

We both turned at the same time to face Perky, who had stood behind us swallowing noisily for some time.

"Mrs Courtenay," he said with great difficulty,"your guests have started to arrive."

She opened her mouth to say something. She changed her mind and swept out of the Blue Suite instead.

"You know, Mr Postlethwaite," I said, "I do not envy Mr Robinson."

"Why not?" asked Perky.

"His bride would have to be a real winner to compensate for a mother-in-law like that."

CHAPTER 6=THE DINNER DATE

I left Pinky in charge of the Courtenay Robinson Wedding. There was no point in remaining as my presence might act as further provocation to the bride's mother.

Left to their own devices the party might generate it's own *bon-homie* as most family parties will. From experience I have learned that man's humanity to his fellow creatures is proportionate to the amount of booze consumed. When the booze is free, man tends to be even more humane. There was a chance that if the wine flowed freely enough even Mrs Courtenay might become more charitable in her assessment of my shortcomings and direct her wrath towards some other unfortunate specimen of mankind.

I decided to forego the courtesy visit that Walter insists should be given to all function organisers. I directed my attention to the other function that was being held in an adjacent suite.

The Young Lions, a pride of 55 earnest shopkeepers, were in an affable mood when I enquired after their collective health and happiness.

They were deeply into mutual admiration for civic chores ably discharged. Congratulations and felicitations abounded and I basked in their approval as the genial host who had provided a venue for such an admirable cause.

It seemed like a good moment to present the account. It was met immediately without cavil and contained a modest bonus for the staff fund.

Mixed fortunes had followed my day so far.

I decided to catch up on some sleep. There would be more problems later on in the day when the overbookings arrived.

I went to my rooms after telling Reception to tell convincing lies to explain my absence. I fell into a deep and dreamless sleep immediately.

The telephone was shrill and insistent. It didn't stop when I swore at it and it didn't go away either.

'Hullo?'

'Personal caller for you, Mr Hammond.' It was Pinky, stand-by receptionist. Slightly miffed Pinky who had lost his half day off. Pain in the arse Pinky who could not go to the Horse of the Year show.

'Hullo?'

'Hi, Martin, is that you?'

It was easy to recognise the voice and accent.

Naomi-Naomi Dwight from Nantucket, Nantucket Island, was not a forgettable girl.

'Hullo, Naomi, how are you?'

Suddenly I didn't resent the intrusion any more.

'Great, Martin, great. How about you?'

'Just woken up. I am O.K. Where are you?'

'Fort William and Troon, Scotland'.

'How long will you be there?' '

'About a week, I guess. Going on to the Highlands then back again to London, England.'

There was a pause. Naomi seemed stuck for words.

'Martin, I just gotta talk to you. There is something I gotta say.'

'Well, fire away then.'

'Martin, I am Sirius.'

'You are?'

'Sure I am.'

'Are you sure?'

'Of course I am. Now listen -when I was staying in your hotel last night I think I behaved very badly and upset you a lot by being disruptive and noisy in the corridor late last night after having a bad time with the guys who were playing poker ……..

I figured it out at last. She meant SERIOUS. Sirius is the Dog Star, Naomi-Naomi was certainly not a dog. The idea amused me and I laughed .

.... and I reckon that you must have a really low opinion of me, Martin, I did behave badly and I wanted you to know that I am really sorry, really sorry for having been a nuisance in your hoteL....
.... Naomi seemed quite happy with her monologue. It didn't need any input from me so I let it flow.
' .... and that really does hurt me a lot, you know, it makes me feel real bad to know that you have such a bad opinion of me.?'

That last bit sounded like a question. Or she was drawing breath.

'I don't have a low opinion of you.' I said.

'You don't?'

'No I don't.'

'You sure about that? I mean, you really are entitled to have a bad opinion about me. When I think about what I was doing last night, I have a really bad opinion about myself, you know?

'Naomi' I said 'I forgive you and pardon you for your transgressions. Just do me one favour, will you?'

'What's that?'

'Don't play poker with strangers. Especially if they are bad losers.'

'Are you fooling with me?' she sounded less serious

'because you really are entitled to have a bad opinion of me, you know?'

'Naomi, once and for all time, be told. I do not have a low opinion of you.'
'
'Cheesus' she said ' it makes me feel real good to hear you say that because I had this notion that you would have this really low opinion of me....... .

'Naomi' I said strongly 'enough of this nonsense. Just believe me when I tell you that I do not hold you in low esteem. You can have a sworn affidavit to that effect if you so desire.'

'Cheees-us' She seemed to be overwhelmed by something. I continued;

'In point of fact, I had proposed to invite you to dinner next time we meet.'

'Would you care to accept my invitation?'

'Would I care to accept?'

'Yes. Would you be my guest for dinner next time we meet?'

'Would I care to accept? You betcha ass I would.'

'Let me know when you are coming back this way again. I will book you a room here and we will dine Chez Louis.'

'Chez who?'

'Chez Louis. He is a friend of mine. He has a restaurant in the country."

'Mardi, baby,' she said 'you are the greatest. I ring you up to apologise and you date me for dinner. Especially when I thought that you would have this really low opinion of me.........................'.

'Naomi-Naomi Dwight' I interrupted ' please don't start all that again. I don't know how to deal with apologies, I wasn't trained for it'.

I was pleasantly wide awake by now. I dressed and went to my office.

The rest of my day passed pleasantly enough. Perky informed me that Mrs Courtenay and her family had bid a tearful farewell to their daughter who had departed for a honeymoon in Bali. He also informed me that Mr Courtenay seemed to be 'a decent sort of chap' and was very understanding about the wedding cake.

A couple of lightweight overbookings gave me an easy time in reception, we had two hundred and fifty sleepers and nearly ninety bums on the Happy Pantry seats.
The bars were up and running well with several dedicated punters witnessing the nightly miracle of turning wine into water.

The regular night manager, Travers, was back on duty after his nights off. This meant that he would cope with all nocturnal troubles and let me sleep undisturbed through the night. I had to conclude that my day had been like the curate's egg – very good in parts.

Tomorrow would bring another crop of problems. Tomorrow I would deal with them.

CHAPTER 7 CASINO CHIPS

Everyone who works for Happy Havens knows that they are in the people business. It is not really forgettable when you are surrounded by people who have expectations which may, or may not, be fulfilled.

I have 80 staff in my Happy Haven. Every day I tour the hotel and greet them all by name in any one of the European languages which we have in common. It makes us both feel good. They can fault my accent, not my intentions. In time we become friends.

And the guests are nearly always pleasant people who will give a courteous reply to a courteous question - provided that you ask the right question in the right place at the right time. Lose this little initiative and you are like the little Dutch boy who took his finger out of the dyke to pick his nose. Suddenly, nobody loves you.

The wrong time to enquire after a guest's health and happiness is when he or she is standing in a queue. I avoid queues in hotels. They are full of people who are impatient. Impatient people can be very rude.

If I am there, they will be rude to me.

I like to lend moral support to my staff when they are under pressure. I like to help them with the bursts of activity that can break out like prairie fires all over the hotel. The problem is, they can usually do their own job far better than I can. My presence does not help much. Sometimes it makes a difficult job even more difficult when I help.

I have found a really useful role for myself. I stand under large signs and repeat what they say.
It works like this; there is a large sign in the reception foyer. It is five metres long and one metre high. It says, in very large letters, RECEPTION. It has an arrow pointing to reception. I stand there until a guest asks" Can you tell me where reception is?" Then I can point the way for him or her.

I was on duty under a large sign which said; 'YOU MAY TELEPHONE FROM HERE' A small anxious man said;
'Can I make a telephone call, please?'

'Yes, of course,' I replied, smiling. I led him three paces to the telephone.

I picked up the receiver to hand it to him just as my lapel bleep shrieked.

He looked at me suspiciously for a moment. Then he decided not to make a call after all. I used the phone to call in to Reception.

'ead office for you, Miss Tammond.'

'Thank you, Ethel, I will take it in my office.' I said.

'Mr Hammond?,' The enquirer from Head Office sounded young. That implied lack of seniority in the hierarchy or else she was fronting for someone with clout.

77

'What can I do to help?'

'Accounts office here. I was asked to ring you to check on progress with your Weekly Return Sheet which has still not arrived.'
'Say again.' I switched instantly from helpful to evasive mode.
'What did you say? I am so sorry, I didn't hear you very well. Must be a bad line.'
Very patiently, she said it all again.

'Oh, yes. The Weekly Return Sheet. We are working on it.'
'Mr Hammond?' she sounded almost apologetic, 'can I please ask you to let me have it right away?'

Who could refuse such a plaintive request and not be considered churlish?
'because my boss gets terribly uptight when I haven't done my summary and he blames me for it.'
'What a rude man he is.' I said unctuously, 'blaming a nice girl like you for someone else's misdeeds.'

'Does that mean that will do it for me right away?'
'Consider it done.' I said.
'Thank you so much' she said.
It would be my Good Deed for the day to make a young woman in Head Office happy.

Every week of my life, on one specific day, I have to face reality. Reality for me is the Weekly Return Sheet. It is inescapable, immutable and unrelenting. Every week it calls for me like the Grim Reaper on a routine visit. I am not free to live out the remainder of my life until the demands of the Weekly Return Sheet are met in full, without equivocation.

An innocent looking spreadsheet, the Weekly Return Sheet is a document of grave importance.

It provides details of all sales achieved and costs incurred during the preceding week. The difference between the two, seasonally adjusted, as they say of the Balance of Trade figures, is my operating profit.

It is meticulously recorded by Ibrahim, my Pakistani Comptroller. It seems to cause little distress to give birth to this document, (the entries are poached directly from in-house sources) but post-natal depression sets in very quickly.
It contains many flaws which emerge under statistical analysis, the modem manager's ball and chain.

Analysis is achieved by an avaricious computer known as Casino Chips. So christened because it is an acronym – Central Hotel Information Processing System – and it earned it's fore name Casino after several spectacular glitches which prompted hysterical tirades from Head Office executives and cynical amusement from the line managers. The root cause of this rage and glee was a diversion of confidential information to unacceptable locations within the group. I was granted a print-out of executive expenses on my terminal under the heading of "Other allowable expenses" which was accessible to all my middle management colleagues. It made really good reading and some deeply caustic remarks were posted anonymously after the event.

Casino Chips lives in Head Office and has attitude. It also has an enormous electronic chip on it's shoulder.

It has an enormous, insatiable appetite for data. which it poaches daily from the terminals in the hotels.

It swallows up all 55 Weekly Return Sheets (which encompass sales and all other local expenditure) copiously and begs for more. It becomes shrill and strident if any small component part of it's data diet is missing. Spiteful e/mails are sent to any suspected defaulters microseconds after the event.

It is unforgiving and unrelenting in it's pursuit of lateness or insufficiency. It is programmed for pessimism. It seeks out sins of omission or commission with more zeal than the Spanish Inquisition under Torquemada's zealous command. It is implacable and it has a grudge against my Happy Haven and me. Every week, without fail, it digests my Weekly Return Sheet and ejaculates several e/mails and a Trading Summary.

Every week, without fail, it seizes upon some aspect of my management and gives it the thumbs down and an electronic raspberry. It compares this year with last year. Budget to date with budget forecast to date. Sleepers, weekly and accumulative. Diners, this week and last week. Functions to date and functions to this same date last year. Somewhere, it probably counts the amount of loo paper used to date and compares it with the amount of loo paper used last year to the same date and draws some sombre conclusion from this.

Casino Chips, if it had a sentient soul, would probably be a depressive, schizoid, suicidal psychopath in need of intensive social re-adjustment.

The Weekly Return Sheet which I had just agreed and sent off to Head Office would not be received passively. Casino Chips would be flexing it's electronic muscles and stretching it's data digestive canal to the limit with that lot in his gullet. I could expect a dyspeptic, bilious and spiteful text and e/mail from him later.

The Head Office of Happy Haven Hotels plc is in Central London. It is the heart and mind of Walter's empire. My lords and masters live their corporate existence there. They conspire against the managers at the sharp end of the business. They plot against each other in Head Office. Walter is the undisputed master of them all, El Supremo, Head Honcho, Lord High Seigneur, the Godhead who must not be denied.

Head Office captains with enough clout are always identified by their initials, never by name. This is one of Walter's idiosyncrasies. He prefers to know his top people by their initials, never by name.

We have a Jaysee. He is my District Manager. He knows all about managing hotels. He is light years older than me and he is not given to compassion, understanding or humanity. His manic pursuit of losses, leakages, deficits and frauds throughout the dozen hotels under his command leaves no space for tolerance or forgiveness. He has the subtlety of a sledgehammer. He is never shy about confrontation. He is my most immediate boss. Others can claim sovereignty over me but I am Jaycees man.

Walter hand-picks his Head Office team. Although not exactly the fruit of his loins, they all bear a certain likeness to Walter. Sober dark suits are *de rigeur* and the paunch and pallor of desk navigators gives uniformity of shape. They ape his formidable frown and the most dedicated sycophants sport goatee beards, just like Walter.
In a behavioural sense they are as one kind. They are drawn together by a mutual affinity, like bears to a honey-pot and vultures to the dead.

Although outwardly benevolent -'just think of us as a service organisation, put there to help you' - their intentions are not wholly charitable. 'We are here to advise you' they say, 'to improve the way in which you run your hotel, for the benefit of the group'.

Like gunboat diplomats, they offer advice which is backed up by a battleship in the bay.

It came as a welcome interruption when the phone rang and it was not Head Office.

'Hi, Martin, how are you?'

My day brightened up as I listened to Naomi- Naomi Dwight chattering away.

'About our dinner date?' I asked eventually.

'Sure thing,' she said 'I've gotten two days, two whole days off next week. Then I leave for Paris, France, Brussels, Belgium and Romiddely with 44 sophomores from Boston Massachusetts. They got the hots for your rope.'

Even if nothing else happened between us, my knowledge of geography would be much improved by association with Naomi-Naomi Dwight from Nantucket, Nantucket Island, Noo England, U.S.of A.

I booked a room for Naomi which was conveniently close to mine. I also arranged for both Pinky and Perky to sleep in the hotel that same night.

Then I reserved a table for two Chez Louis'.

The day of my dinner date with Naomi had some peaks and some troughs.

The good parts were very good. The punters were happy and the staff sounded as though they really meant it when they said "Have a nice day". Several block bookings from Head Office made the diary look good. A couple of weddings and a society dinner came through after much competitive scratching.

An annual wage increase for all employees had been agreed with Happy Havens. The sun was shining on us all.

Two clouds on the horizon foretold a deteriorating climate to come. Casino Chips had produced a report on my Happy Haven full of spiteful and odious comparisons. My District Manager, Jaysee, wanted to talk to me about this report. With typical candour and absent subtlety, Jaysee had said;

"Hammond, you are making a balls up. I will see you on Friday morning at 8 a.m. to talk about it."

I put all this out of my mind when I took Naomi to a little restaurant in the country known as 'Chez Louis.'

'Louis' was a free adaptation of the proprietor's name. He was christened Llewelyn. Of irrepressible Welsh stock, Louis had discovered a basic truth many years ago.

He realised, intuitively, that selling food to people who are already hungry is an extension of showmanship.

He had acquired this wisdom and a mock European accent whilst working for Happy Haven Hotels as a banquetting manager. We had been friends for many years. I envied him his freedom from authority. He envied my freedom from debt.

Louis had purchased his restaurant from the disenchanted previous owners at considerably less than cost.

'Chez Louis' had risen from the ashes of their dream of a rural idyll far away from the metropolitan rat race. It had taken them two years of unrelenting effort and half their capital to learn that commercial success follows the greedy, not the good.

Louis had timed his shrewd offer to perfection. Depressed by their auditors, harried by their bankers and doomed by an economic downturn they had caved in and fled back gratefully to the city.

"Monsieur" he said' and "Madame."

With an elaborate gesture he pulled a chair for Naomi and flicked it with his serviette in one graceful flourish. He put his hand on his heart and gazed at Naomi adoringly.
 Then he sighed heavily. He joined thumb to finger and kissed them noisily before he leaned over to adjust my knife and fork.

"Big improvement on the last scrubber you brought here, Marty, buoyo."

Louis recommended the meal, which we ate without demur. He enjoyed the freedom of my Happy Haven and I enjoyed the freedom of his restaurant. The question of cost never arose. It is called hospitality if you entertain clients and is an allowable expense. The same largesse applies to friends.

'How's your job going?' asked Naomi towards the end of the meal.
'Just at the moment,' I said 'I am in trouble with my Head Office.'

'Why so?'

;My figures and percentages are all wrong.'

'Who says so?'

'My boss, Jaysee.'

'Is that his name?'

'All my bosses are known by their initials. They don't have names.'

'So he is Jesus Christ?'

'In a way, yes. He is not often wrong. He expects the same of me.'

'Will he give you a bad time?'

'We meet this Friday. I will know after that. I don't think he will be easy on me.'

'What does he expect from you?'

'More of everything. Bigger and better profits.'

'He sounds like a real sonofabitch.'

'He is. If I am still around after Friday, there may be some pieces left to pick up.'

'I'll still be around' she said, 'and if that bastard gives you a real bad time, baby, I
will tear him apart and scatter the pieces around.'

She clawed the air between us with finger nails painted a fashionable shade of chicken liver brown.

'I'm glad we are on the same side.' I said with feeling. Naomi's capacity for inflicting grievous bodily harm on men was beginning to worry me. I had seen her in action before.

'How about you, Naomi, have you got any plans of your own?'

'I did have. But they changed some.' When Naomi was serious, her face took on a strange and haunting look. Sadness just did not belong there.

'Tell me about it.'

'It began about a year ago. I came over from the States for a spell in Europe. I love it here. It's great. I really belong here, like it's my own country and I was having a ball every day of my life.'

'So what went wrong?'

'Would you believe," she said vehemently "that I am the world's number one sucker? Would you really believe that?'

'No, I wouldn't.'

'Well I am.'

'Naomi, sweetheart,' I said, 'you do not strike me as a vulnerable lass. Just the opposite, really. Quite capable of taking care of yourself.' I had a brief recall of a former guest swaying away from her, moaning softly and holding his crotch.

'I figure that means you really do believe I am a sucker. And you are right. I am.'

'Tell me about it,' I said 'then we can decide who is right.'

'Like I said;' Naomi had a *raconteuse* style that any interviewer would envy, 'everything was going great for me. My job, my friends, my life, everything was AOK. I was happy. You know what happiness is, Mardy?'

'I've got my own version of it.'

'So with everything going great for me, what do you think I did?'

'I can't imagine,' I said, 'but I know you are going to tell me.'

'I blew it' she said, 'boy, I really blew it.'

'You did?'

She nodded vigourously;

' Yes. I really blew it.'

'What did you blow?'

'Everything,' she said, 'I blew it all away.'

'Somewhere along that line' I said, 'you lost me.'

'Always, always' she said, shaking her head, 'just as soon as things are going great for me, I blow it.

And there is always some man to help me along and get me really messed up.'

'Are you telling me, Naomi, that you had an unhappy love affair? Is that what you are saying?'

'It sounds simple when you say it like that," she said softly, "but when you are in there it is hell.- a really bad place to be.'

'Some men are real bastards' I said sanctimoniously.

'You are right about that' she said intensely, 'and I swore to myself that I would never, ever fall in love again.'

'And is this the first time you have ever said that?' I asked.

She treated me to a long, level stare. It was either complete loathing or unbridled passion that came across. One day I hope to be able to tell the difference between the two extremes. I need more practice still.

'Have you ever been in love? I mean really deeply, truly in love?' she asked.

'I thought I was in love several times' I said, 'but it turned out to be lust.'

That look came across the table at me again, so I added;

'But it is probably because I haven't yet met the kind of woman who would have that effect on me. Not yet, anyway.'

'Then you just cannot know what it is like.'

'Would you like to tell me about the man you used to love but now hate?'

This suggestion seemed to cheer her up a little. She leaned forward dramatically.

'This is the first time I have ever spoken about it to anyone. But my shrink always told me to talk my problems out, so I guess it's gotta be you.'

'You have my undivided attention,' I said.

'Everything was going really well for me when I came over here. I had friends. I was adjusted. I was seeing straight for the first time in years. My life made a lotta sense. I went to parties, real parties, no bad scenes with liquor or drugs or anything like that, just music and people and fun. My job was great, I travelled a lot and it was always good to be back.'

'Then one week-end I went to a house party in the country. At a country club, with swimming, horse-back riding, golf and all. We had a ball there and it was terrific.'

'I met this guy there' she said ruefully,'and I was zapped. Like I've never been zapped before.'

She studied her finger nails intently. Then she looked up. 'I've always had this hang-up about older men, you know?'

I nodded sympathetically and she said; 'This one stepped straight down from my favourite fantasy. He was very British and you know that just knocks me out, Mardy, you really do know that?'

It sounded like a question so I nodded encouragement.
'Anyway, he showed me around, and he really showed me a good time, so we started dating when we both got back to town afterwards.'

'We even talked divorce and marriage.'

'And then the crunch came?' I asked.

She nodded. 'I kept telling myself that it would'nt work out with someone old enough to be my father and already married. But It wasn't a time for good sense. I loved that man so much it hurt. It still does hurt a bit when I think about him.'

'How long since the break up?'

'I really knew that it was coming for about three month' she said sadly 'but I did'nt want to face it. The flowers, the phone calls, the dates all started to slow up a little and by the end even his secretary would give me the kiss off when I called him. Then finally he took me out to the theatre and dinner and I just knew it was curtains for him and me.'

'What did he say to you?' I asked. It was a question not wholly without relevance to a single man.

'He told me about his wife, his kids, his responsibilities. All the things that men tell you about when they are giving you the brush off.'

I made a mental note of that.

'And do you know what really pissed me off and choked me in the end, Mardy?, What really put the kiss of death on the whole relationship?'

'No. Tell me?'

'Money,' she said decisively. 'Money. The bastard offered to give me money. Like he was buying me off.' She shook her head.

'What a bastard' I said 'how much did he offer?'

Either she did not hear me or she ignored me.

'All that was more than three months ago. Ever since I have worked hard to forget it and put it out of my mind '

'Suddenly' she said brightly, 'I feel a whole lot better about it. I guess my shrink was right.Problems should be talked out.'

'The day will come, Naomi-Naomi Dwight,' I said 'when you will be able to walk straight up to him, call him a bastard and spit right in his eye.'

'Oh boy,' said Naomi, 'I would really enjoy that. I could call him a bastard, pull his cute little goatee beard and spit right in his eye.'

'How about,' I suggested 'a right knee in the balls? That is something you do really well.'

'Right on.' she said with enthusiasm, 'if I was close enough to pull his beard and spit in his eye, I could knee him in the balls at the same time.'

Naomi's potential for emasculation was beginning to worry me even more, so I suggested;

'Why not just ring him up and call him a bastard?'

'Yeah, I could do that,' Naomi said, ' I know his number by heart'.

Naomi recited the telephone number that she knew by heart. I could not think of any single good reason at all to tell her that it was the telephone number of Happy Havens Head Office.

CHAPTER 8 CONFRONTATION

I was scheduled to meet Jaysee at 8.00a.m. on Friday in my office to discuss my trading results. I arrived at 7.55.a.m. Jaysee was already there. He was sitting on my side of the desk. Sombre as a Hanging Judge, melancholy as a Bassett hound, he pointed to the chair opposite himself.

'Sit down, Hammond.' he said 'and Good Morning.'
'I trust you are well?' he said, oozing insincerity.

 Without waiting for a reply he produced my last Weekly Report. 'That was your last chance to make good, Hammond" he said " and you made a right balls of it. What went wrong?'

'Which part in particular? ' I asked defensively.

Jaysee is not a man who minces his words. He prefers the full frontal, uncluttered approach.

'The whole sodding lot.' he said.

'Can we take it bit by bit?' I suggested.

He made powerful negative waves. 'Last week your occupancy ratio was 54.5%. The previous year it was 62.5%. Your accumulative to date is 58.3%. The budget cumulative is 61.9%. Last year it was 2.1 % over budget at 62.7% '

He didn't look down once whilst reciting these figures. They were branded on his memory.

He glared at me.

'We seem to be very full every night.' I said lamely.

'Not full enough." he growled, ' and it is your week-ends that are letting you down. Get 'em in at week-ends and the weekdays will look after themselves.'

"I can't just drag them in off the street," I said, "I need some help from marketing now and then."

'You get more than enough help from marketing. They send the majority of the bookings here. You get all the overspill from other hotels in the district. You are the only one with the space.' he said nastily.

'But I don't get any week-end bookings from Marketing" I said "and I only get the overbookings from other hotels.'

With a dismissive wave Jaysee said ;
'Overbookings are a fact of life. You have to live with them.'

'You should get up off your arse, Hammond, go out into the market place and sell the empty space' Jaysee said passionately, 'that it what it is all about, selling into the low periods, filling the gaps on the chart, getting the punters in, putting heads on pillows and bums on seats and keeping the house full.'

His voice had risen to a controlled bellow and we had only just started.

'That's all very well,' I said, 'but just where am I supposed to find all these weekenders to fill the place up? People aren't clamouring to come here just because it is outer London, you know.'

I had thought that one out well in advance. I had considered it be a real cannonball of logic. Jaysee parried it easily.
"Just for starters, Hammond" he grated 'in my patch this weekend there are eight Art Appreciation Seminars, four Antique teach-ins, three Folk Music get togethers, two Motor Rallies and two Catholic pray-ins. Everyone, except you, has got something going this week-end. And they all bring in the punters."

"I've got the Annual Fruiterers Association Dinner" I said proudly.

'Peanuts' said Jaysee in disgust, ' you should do them on a week day.'

'And I've got the Natural Childbirth Classes here as well.' I offered.

'Expectant mothers,' replied Jaysee with heavy logic, 'do not stray far from their homes. They are not good spenders.'

'I've had a preliminary meeting with U.K.I.P' I said
'That's all we need," said Jaysee ;'
'A U.K.I.P.Conference here!'

'It is good business' I said
'They are big spenders. They will be here from Friday until Sunday night.'

'Put it out of your mind, Hammond. Every other hotel in the district has already turned them down. They cause riots, civil disorder and criminal assemblies.'

'Any hotel that accepts them may not be in business by the following Monday.'

'Well' I said, 'there's always the League for Same sex Marriage.'

Jaysee's selective prejudice apparently did include gays.

'Might be worth considering,' he muttered, 'but why the hell can't you sell the ordinary punters who like Antiques, Folk Music, Poetry, Motor Rallies, Sunday League Football, Cricket and Pray-ins instead of Fascist hard-nuts and kinky perverts?"

His blood pressure was rising again. I said;

'How about a Chess Conference?'

'Don't just think about it, Hammond' he roared, 'organise yourself and sell it!'

'I just don't seem to get enough time.' I said.

'Make time, Hammond.' said Jaysee, leaning towards me, 'organise yourself, get ahead of yourself, plan your day so that you don't cover the same ground twice. Make sure that your Heads of Department know what it's all about. Save yourself five minutes very day. Don't just shove off and do nothing with the time you save. Use the time to sell the hotel. Then increase the amount of time you save every day until you spend at least one hour every day selling into the low patches. That's what hotel management is all about, Hammond, and the sooner you realise it the better for us all.'

I got the impression that someone else had said there wasn't enough time in the day to Jaysee before. This was his standard reply.

'Would you like some coffee?' I asked.

'No' he replied, 'and you are going to need a block booking every week-end from now to year end to get back on target. Will you make it?'

I put on my pensive executive frown.

'I may have a little difficulty there' I said.
'Damn right you will,' snarled Jaysee. 'I have already looked at your Forward Booking Diary. It is as bare as a badger's arse.'

'There are one or two events which might come through' I said, 'but not enough to keep us full from now to year end.'

Jaysee glared at the ceiling balefully.

'Bloody lightweights' he fumed 'why do they always give me the bloody lightweights and wankers.'

He looked at me. He spoke gently, but his expression was pained. He looked like a tiger with toothache;

'Hammond' he said, 'do you know what is involved in changing a budget forecast?'

'No' I said, completely misled by his soothing manner, 'but I would like to know.'

Jaysee nodded, his lips pursed like a rosebud.

'You make an appointment to see Emen in Finance. He is a condescending bastard and he will give me the standard 15 minute spiel about over optimism when preparing forecasts. Then he will look at my amendments to district consolidated forecast and tell me of the difficulty of amending his group-consolidated forecast against my renewed projections and the impact it will have on the company's expectations which is a matter for the attention of our chairman and chief executive. Have you got that?'

'Yes' I lied, 'quite so.'

'And then' said Jaysee, 'I have to attend the Budgetary Review Committee Meeting.'

'Really' I said.

'Yes, really' he said, ' and I have to explain it all over again. They ask exactly the same questions as Emen and I have to give exactly the same answers. Then they go into a huddle. When they come out of it they ask a few more stupid questions. Then they tell me that they are treating this as an exception and caution me to be better prepared next time.' He didn't even draw breath before continuing;

'Of course, it makes me look very foolish. And I don't like that Hammond. I don't like that at all.' He still spoke quietly and without rancour.

'And all because one of my unit managers just cannot find enough time to sell his hotel at weekends.' He sighed and shook his head.

'Does'nt it make you feel very small, Hammond, to know that you are the cause of so much bother to me ?'

I had to admit that it did.

'You are a wanker, Hammond, a bloody lightweight wanker.' He said it in a casual, relaxed way, as if talking to his favourite dog.

I wished I had Pinky's habit of writing everything down. It created time for dredging up convincing answers.

'Before I start my inspection of the hotel, Hammond, which I have no doubt will exceed my worst expectations, there is the matter of the bars result to discuss.'

'Ah yes, the bars result. I am not entirely happy about that.'

'Then at least we agree about something.'

I ignored his sarcasm.

'It is the gradual shift in the sales mix and the changeable nature of the surplus that concerns me.' That is an example of the jargon of senior managers when they confer together.

'Granted you have noticed the trend, Hammond, but what have you been doing about it?' replied Jaysee, trying very hard to debase the executive coinage.

'I discuss the result with the bars manager .'

'And?'

'He is at a loss to explain it.'

'Why do you think he can't explain it?'

'Because he is just as puzzled as I am by the result.'

'And you believe him?'

'Yes. what other explanation could there be?'

'Hammond,' said Jaysee softly, 'never, ever trust a barman. If a man is born honest he does'nt become a barman. A monk. maybe, or a magistrate, but never a barman.'

'What do you think is going down then?'

'Thieving,' said Jaysee 'thieving and robbery.'

'But surely ....'

Jaysee raised his hand, commanding silence. He snapped up a finger.

'One' he said, 'the sales mix is changing.'

'Two' another finger went up, 'your surplus is growing larger.'

'Three' he waggled three fingers, 'the sales mix has been constant here for three years. I know because I looked it up.'

If Jaysee said that he had looked up the records for the past three years then I believed him.

'That paints a picture,' he said 'of skulduggery.'

'It does?'

'Yes. He is bringing in his own bottles and selling his own booze in your bar and pocketing the cash.'

I felt a leaden depression in my middle. I had spent hours listening to the bars manager and his convincing stories. I had trusted him and that trust had been betrayed.

'Damn the bastard,' I said it with feeling,

'I will kill him for this.'

'No you won't,' said Jaysee, 'you will catch him first.'

'How?'

'Mark every bottle in the cellar, but not on the label. Then spot check the bars for any bottle which does not carry your mark.'

'And then I can prosecute him with that as evidence?'
'You catch him, Hammond' said Jaysee heavily, 'I'll prosecute him.'
It was the first note of happiness that I had detected in him since we met.

'I'll catch him for you.' I promised, completely underestimating my opponent.

I got up to lead Jaysee on his tour of inspection. 'We haven't discussed the food result yet,' he said " and there are some letters of complaint as well.'
The lesser of these two evils was the food.

'I'm pretty sure .that I can get on top of the food result here.' I said.

'Judging from the results achieved, Hammond, you couldn't get on top of a molehill.'

'How many?' I asked, 'of your units are on target with food?' I knew I was on firm ground there. I had rung up half a dozen other Happy Haven managers to ask about food results.

'Very, very few,' said Jaysee, 'but I will give you one guess who is the worst of a bad bunch.'
'The kind of operation that you run here, Hammond, should guarantee you a full house. It should be the bargain basement give-away of a lifetime. The value for money that your punters get here should put every restaurant in the district out of business. Your Pantry should be full to bursting all the time. And is it full all the time Hammond?'

'Well, not exactly full.' I said.

'Damn right it isn't,' roared Jaysee, 'because the food never gets onto the plate in the first place. It disappears," he shouted, "before it ever gets that far.'

'But surely ....'
'I am a reasonable man, Hammond, a reasonable man doing a reasonable job to the best of my ability.'

He smiled at me grimly, the way Public Executioners do.

'But I will not tolerate a nest of thieves in my patch'who make Ali-Baba look like an amateur.'

'The security on food here............... .'

'Is bloody awful.' Jaysee finished the sentence for me.

He produced a large unopened tin of orange juice, the cooked tail end of a salmon, a shrivelled turkey leg, half a packet of sliced bacon, some tea bags and the remnants of a sliced loaf.
He laid these items on my desk with precision.
They came from his brief case.

'Where?' he said, 'do you think that I found these?'

I shook my head. He re-arranged the items deftly, like an old fashioned grocer displaying his wares.

'This tin of orange juice,' he tapped the top lightly, 'I found in the dry food store.'
'Do you know how I managed to find it there, Hammond?'

I shook my head again, stifling a provocative suggestion.

'Very, very easily,' he said. 'I just walked in and picked it up.'

'And then I walked out again, no trouble at all. I just walked in and walked out again with whatever I wanted. No body asked me what I was doing there, whether I had the right to be there or not. Nobody made any attempt to stop me. I suppose nobody bothered because they can pop in or out any time they feel like it. If they don't find what they are looking for first time, they can just pop back later after it has been delivered.'

'I gave strict instructions' I said, 'that the dry stores were to be kept locked at all times.'
"Instructions!" Jaysee snarled, "you gave instructions?"

'Who the hell do you think you are dealing with? Lawyers?'

"No of course not,' I said crossly, 'but. .... ".

'Thieves!' Jaysee roared, 'thieves. That's who you are dealing with. And they are robbing you blind. From this moment on, Hammond, just keep the stores locked. If you can't trust anybody with the keys issue all the stores yourself. Understand?'

'And now to the next item' Jaysee cooed,' the tea-bags, bacon and sliced bread.'

He made it sound like an indictable offence.
'I will not bore you with petty details such as where I found them,' he said 'I'll just concentrate on the fact that they shouldn't have been there to begin with.'

That was one of my favourite treats knocked on the head. Ethel could make superb bacon sarnies and mugs of steaming hot tea from a small stove hidden under the Reception desk.

'O.K.' I said, 'life will be a little bleaker without treats, but it won't happen again.'

Jaysee drew a sharp breath. 'Staff canteens, Hammond, are supplied at considerable expense for staff to take meals in. It should not be necessary,' he said with great emphasis, 'for staff to exist on bacon butties and tea brewed illicitly under the Reception desk. All meals, I repeat all meals, will be taken in the proper place from now on.'

'I will see to it.' I said.

'It is a well known fact, Hammond,' Jaysee rumbled on his elephantine way, 'that you can learn as much about a hotel by going in the back door as you can by going in the front door.' I nodded. 'And do you know why you can learn as much about a hotel by going in the back door as you can by going in the front door?'

I shook my head. 'Because,' said Jaysee,' that is where everything is chucked away.'
He was trying to make a point. A very laboured one, but a point just the same.

'Where everything is chucked away?' I said.
The repetition and heavy silence that followed was pure voodoo. When I could stand it no longer, I asked; 'And what did you find there?'

'I'm glad you asked me that, Hammond.' said Jaysee, giving his sardonic impression of gladness, 'because it brings me to the next two items, the salmon and the turkey.'

A large forefinger shaped like a raw pork sausage dabbed softly on the salmon scales. He lifted it to his nose and inhaled deeply.

'Now this salmon' he said, 'is almost certainly a farm salmon. A fair fish,' he said with approval, ' probably cooked yesterday. Not in the same league as a Dee salmon caught with rod and line, but a fair fish none the less. It deserves respect, Hammond, and understanding. Which is precisely what it did not find here. It was in the swill bin.'

'It was probably plate waste.' I said.

"Oh no it wasn't. It hadn't been portioned." Jaysee was warming to his theme nicely.

'What do you mean?'

'This cut of salmon,' he said, waving it towards me, 'is the tail-end. When you come to the end of a salmon, you can't cut it into steaks any more. Prudent and wise chefs will cut it into two flats which are very attractive and tasty.'

'Imprudent chefs, however,' he said 'are in too much of a hurry to bother with such niceties. They just chuck it into the swill bin and give their managers a very low food percentage.'

'In fact, Hammond,' his voice was rising again, 'it belongs almost anywhere except the swill bin.'

'I just don't know how that happened,' I said, 'the chef here is very good ..... .'

'Then maybe, Hammond,' Jaysee gave me his alarming smile again 'you can tell me how this turkey drumstick came to be keeping it company?'

I was not falling into the trap of saying anything this time.

'Then I will tell you how it came about." he said.

"Time was,' he said ruefully, 'when turkeys were prepared properly. We used to take out the wishbone, pull the tendon out of the legs, then scorch and truss the whole carcass before they ever went near to the oven.' Nowadays,' he said sadly, 'they come deep frozen in plastic bags. So-called chefs just shove them straight into a convection oven and leave them there all afternoon, six or ten at a time. They don't have the wit, nous or motivation to cook them properly. The first chef back in the evening pulls them out of the convection oven, blasted to a cinder.'

'I have never seen turkeys cooked during the afternoon here.'

'Cooked they are,' said Jaysee, 'but very badly cooked. And one of the symptoms of this method of cooking is the shrivelled leg with dark blue flesh and separated tendons.'

He made it sound like gallows bait.

'Just like this.' He handed the turkey drumstick to me with mock courtesy. I was wandering what to do with all the illicit produce which was spread all over my desk when Jaysee said; 'No system of control ever works without thought and judgment, Hammond.'

He nodded in approval, swayed by this borrowed bit of wisdom.

'What is needed here is more supervision, more communication, more dialogue between people and departments. Get all your people together, Hammond, and tell them exactly what you expect from them.'

'Motivate them' he snarled, 'motivate them to do a better job quicker!'

'We do have staff meetings here, you know.'

'And just what do you discuss on these rare occasions,' asked Jaysee. 'staff uniforms and staff food? Rates of pay and time off?'

He seemed to have covered it in one. Those were the main and prevailing topics at all my staff meetings.
'We do talk about other things" I said.

'I will look at the minutes later.' he replied, laying the foundations for another disputed.

'We had better start the tour of inspection, Hammond.' he growled at me.

'Shall I lead?.' I asked innocently. Maybe he had forgotten about the letters of complaint.

The public Jaysee was a different person to the private Jaysee.

Within the privacy of my office he was a tiger. He had roared and slashed at me, inflicting some nasty wounds which would take a long time to heal.

Away from my office, in the hotel, he was a pussycat. He purred, he moved sleekly, he smiled. He made little jokes softly, and he said he was very pleased to meet everyone. He remembered the names of several long serving staff. He walked towards them with a broad smile and outstretched hand. He enquired after everyone's health and took an intense interest in the reply. He spoke of his own family, growing up and coping with similar problems. He smiled, he nodded, he approved. He touched the upper arm of all the girls gently as he spoke to them.

'Such a nice man,' they all sighed as he strode away, 'so kindly and considerate.'

Warm and positive waves followed us everywhere on a triumphal whistle-stop tour. Jaysee was way ahead on brownie points. Even Iceberg melted a little in a warm encounter with her District Manager. She said that she thought she could detect a slight improvement in the linen-hire firm.

The Bars manager, whose wits had been honed to fine edge by a thousand similar encounters had a jovial Queensbury rules round with Jaysee. It was a draw.

Chef, stumbling through the English language undergrowth, finally understood the question. 'Ja. Ja,' he said 'in the afternoon we do cook the turkiss, ya.'

The Restaurant manager was on leave from melancholia after a modest, unexpected win at the local race -track. He forgot his fallen arches and duodenum long enough to instruct Jaysee how to fold serviettes in such a way that Walter was even more prominent than usual.

Pinky and Perky tried not to stand to attention when addressed collectively by Jaysee. They failed. Their only contribution to the dialogue was;

'Thank you, sir.' and 'Yessir.'

Finally, Ethel received a really flattering comment from Jaysee that made her blush deep in sunset patches to her slender throat. Then we were back in my office again.

Throughout the tour, I had bathed in the glow of Jaysee's approval. He did not usurp or undermine my authority. He steered all matters of administration and protocol deftly back to me.

'That really is a matter for Mr Hammond' he had said gently on several occasions, 'I feel sure that he will find the time to discuss it with you later.'

'How about it, Martin?' he had said, ' can you find the time to talk it over with our friend here?'

To which I have to reply, 'Of course I can! Let's meet later.'

But the tiger was back in his borrowed lair the moment the door of my office closed.

"That bars manager of yours," he said shaking his head slowly, "I have seen straighter corkscrews."

"He's a wily sod, all right." I said.

'He is going to be one tricky bugger to catch,' said Jaycee ' and you will have to get up very early in the morning to trap him.'

'Don't you worry,' I said bravely 'I will get him for you.'

'And as for chef,' he shook his head sadly, 'you still have a long way to go there.'

'I will keep a close eye on him,'

I was hoping that the mood of joviality and bonhomie which went with our tour of the hotel would last. He had been in the hotel for several hours. With luck he would be ready to leave soon.

But he settled comfortably behind my desk and scowled at the produce which was still on display. The salmon was beginning to curl at the edges and hum a bit. The twisted remnants of the turkey drumstick was still in place. It looked like a pastiche of man's inhumanity to man.

'It all needs pulling together' he said, 'too many loose ends hanging out. The feel of the place is all wrong.'
'What is needed here,' he mused with fingers arched ' is firm management that can get on top of the place and pull it all together.'

I got the impression that he was talking to someone else. Someone much higher up the corporate tree.

'Stronger marketing is a must.' he said "but before the place can be sold, it needs more discipline and control.'

'A good shake-up,' he said 'that is what it really needs. Rattle the cage a bit.'

He focussed on me and frowned.
'Time was, Hammond,' he said 'when you could give a manager one month to sort it or else.'

He seized himself by the throat and bulged his eyes.

'But we can't do that any more,' he said sadly, 'we have to behave as though our balls have been cut off. You can't just fire people like we did in the good old days. Even if they are useless wankers.'

I made appropriate regretful noises.

'So I must boost your miserable performance here. I will have to bring in the Wrecking Crew. They will get the marketing moving and sort the place out once and for all.'

'Given a fair wind and good judgment,' he said 'they might be able to repair some of the damage and get the place back on target by the end of the year.'

I went pale at the thought of the Wrecking Crew stamping all over my hotel in their size 12 boots. Their reputation went before them throughout the group.

If Jaysee meant to frighten me, he had succeeded.

The Wrecking Crew are a team of four experts. They were known by their function, not by name or initials. Marketing. Food and Beverage. Control. Liaison. Like the four Horsemen of the Apocalypse.

At their best, they were the busy and able group of men who supervised the opening and start-up of new hotels.

At their worst they were the sinister, self-assured team who came from Head Office. They were on intimate terms with everyone in Head Office. Their mission was to remove unacceptable deviation from the will of Walter. They were not unassuming men dedicated to their task. They were Walter's hit men who punished sins of omission and commission with equal severity.

'sOf course,' said Jaysee, 'you will need the full team here. I will find out when they are free. It won't be for some time yet. They are doing another assignment for me. That will take some time yet.'

It was comforting to know that some other hotel in Jaysee's patch was being turned over by the Wrecking Crew. Maybe it would blunt their teeth a little.

Jaysee started to pack his brief case. I conducted a brief internal debate on raising some objections to the Wrecking Crew visit. Further discussion would risk Jaysee coming back to the letters of complaint which had slipped off the agenda somehow. To duck the issue might speed his departure.
Jaysee looked at his diary.

'I am going to send you on a course, Hammond.' he announced.

'What sort of course?'

'Not a course of remedial treatment, Hammond' he said, 'from which you would derive enormous benefit. A course on Food and Beverage Control run by Head Office.'

'When?'

'As soon as I can arrange it.'
This idea seemed to be less sinister than the one about the Wrecking Crew.
'Who will run the hotel when I am away?'

He was still packing his brief case when he said;
'How many staff do you have here, Hammond?'

'80. When we are fully staffed.'

'They won't even miss you.' he said nastily.

'Before I go,' he added ' I am leaving three letters for you to report on. One is from a solicitor who claims damages for a client whose confirmed booking went wrong. The second is from a lady whose daughter's wedding was fouled up by a missing cake. The third is from a punter who says he was charged £125 for damages to a room that he did not cause. Let me have your reply by the end of the week, Hammond.'

He left briskly, pausing only to speak to the receptionist. He was smiling broadly and touched her upper arm lightly as he spoke.

Then Jaysee left my hotel to persecute some other minority group in another part of his patch.

He left behind a scared manager whose scattered wits were returning very slowly to base. When I held out my left hand, all the fingers trembled in unison.

This was an improvement. Earlier on they had all trembled randomly. Sweat had dried on my body like scales. I needed a shower to scour away some of the staleness.

But even more than that, I needed someone to talk to, to confide in. Someone who would listen to me with sympathy and understanding, listen to my point of view. Someone who would be supportive and give me good advice.

It was clear that Jaysee wanted me out. If I wrote my letter of resignation right away, he would accept it.

Then he could send the Wrecking Crew in to manage the hotel until my successor arrived.
I had been guilty of over-confidence. I should have anticipated his arrival and prepared myself more thoroughly. I could have headed off some of his attack with better homework. If I got another chance, I would put up a much better defence.

He had taken me by surprise that time. It wouldn't happen again.

But maybe that was my last chance. If Jaysee had decided to force me out, my chances of staying were slim. He outranked me by a mile and he was much nastier. He could conspire with Casino Chips to make my results appear really, really bad. He could put it about that I was a lightweight wanker who needed propping up. He conducted my appraisal every year and he could make that look horrendous.

But there was something puzzling in there. Why send me on a course if he wanted me to leave?

That would be expensive and unnecessary. It couldn't be justified on economic grounds. And what about his scheme to trap the bars manager? That was also forward facing. Why make plans for the future if you haven't got one?

I remembered a lesson from the past which stated "Never resign. Wait until you are fired." There was sound logic in there. Probably, I should think it all through more thoroughly before doing anything drastic....... .

'I fought you might like coffee.'

Ethel crystalised in front of me like a figure from the fog. She put a tray of coffee and biscuits on my desk.

'Thank you Ethel,' I said, 'that was a kind thought.'

She looked at me quizzically, her brows knitted in maternal concern.

'You all right, Miss Tammond?'

'Yes, I'm O.K.'

'Are you sure? You look a bit funny to me.'

'I just got thrashed by my boss.'

Ethel looked at my desk. Jaysee's trophies were still on it.

'I'll get rid of all this rubbish.' she said briskly. The trophies were swept into the waste paper basket with brisk efficiency.

'I hope you didn't get into trouble with Jaysee about the bread and bacon.'

'No. He just said it was a fire risk cooking under the desk.'

'You can't argue with that, can you?'

'I wouldn't argue with 'im. Not with the Taliban,' she said.

'Is that what you call him? The Taliban.'

'That's because he is a miserable bugger who doesn't like anybody to enjoy themselves.'

'Ah well.' I said 'no more bacon sarnies for you and I.;

She smiled at me mischieviously.

'No more bacon sarnies, Boss. We will have to settle for chocolate biscuits instead,won't we?'

Maybe Ethel was right. Jaysee was just a miserable bugger who did not like to see people enjoying themselves. I ate a chocolate biscuit and drank some coffee.

Pinky and Perky must have been hovering near to my office. They appeared almost immediately when I rang the Reception Office.

'Gentlemen,' I said, 'it would appear that we have a problem in this hotel.'

I stared hard at both of them and paused for a long time. Jaysee had done that to me and it had made me feel very uncomfortable.

Pinky cracked first.

'What sort of problem?'

'The problem here is caused by lightweight assistant managers who are wankers.'

That went down like a lead balloon. Neither moved or spoke. Something more was called for.

'What is needed here is strong management who can get on top of the place and sort out all the loose ends whilst selling into the low spots.'

When I listened to my own words they didn't make a lot of sense. Jaysee had been much more forceful and convincing.

My audience was unmoved. Perky's adam's apple was bobbing up and down but no words came out. Pinky's notebook was ready.

'The place has been allowed to deteriorate to such an extent that we are to be turned over by the Wrecking Crew.'

I must have lacked Jaysee's derogatory style. My audience registered stony indifference.

'What have you got to say to that?' I asked, hoping for a response.

Perky was trying very hard to say something. I waited anxiously.

'Someone has pinched a can of orange juice from the stores.'

'When?'

'This morning,' he said, 'just before you started your tour with the District Manager.'

'Why didn't you tell me sooner?'

'I didn't think it was important enough.'

'Who told you?'

'Chef. He turned his back for a second and someone went into the stores.'

I shook my head slowly.

'Doesn't it make you feel very small, Mr Postlewaite to know that you are so much bother to me?'

Judging from the expression on his face, it didn't.

'From this moment on,' I said, imitating Jaysee's bark, 'keep the keys in your pocket and supervise all issues yourself.'

'Is that the missing tin of orange juice on your desk?' he asked.

'Yes it is. Just put it back in the stores.' I said in despair.

'What about me? Is there something I can do, too?'

Pinky had his notebook open. He looked like a puppy waiting for a stick to be thrown.

I wasn't getting through to them. They just were not afraid of me. I definitely needed more practice at scaring people. Maybe I could go on a course and learn how to scare people witless.

One last try, I thought. In my gruff voice I said;

"There are three letters of complaint from punters who have had a bad time here.
Let me have a written report on all of them by the end of the week."

'Gosh, thanks,' he replied. 'thank you very much.'

I tried to detect sarcasm in his tone. It wasn't there.

Left alone, I concentrated on my part of the plan. I had to trap the bars manager. Jaysee had said that he was bringing in his own bottles of booze and selling it over the bar. Then he pocketed the cash for himself. He had to be caught in the act. I had to produce the evidence. That would come from bottles which did not belong in the bar.

If I marked all the bottles before they arrived in the bar, any bottle which did not carry my marker would be proof of dishonesty. "Don't mark the label," Jaysee had said, "because the label can come off."

'Mark the bottle itself with something permanent.'

I set off for the cellar with an indelible marker.

'You catch him, Hammond. I will prosecute him.' Jaysee's words echoed through my memory

'I'll catch him for you, Jaysee,' I said out loud, 'my job depends on it.'

CHAPTER 9 THE SEMINAR

One Happy Haven Hotel is very much like another. More like identical twins than brothers. They are built that way deliberately. Punters are supposed to relax more in familiar surroundings. Walter smiles on all his guests, everywhere, with equal familiarity.

I was a guest in another hotel. A delegate to a course on Food and Beverage Control, warmly recommended by my boss, Jaysee.

When hotel managers stay in another manager's hotel, they face two choices. Either you ignore everything that goes on about you. Or you run the hotel yourself, like a back seat driver. When my colleagues and friends stay at my Happy Haven, I am happier when they keep their heads down. That is what I decided to do.

A pleasant note from the course tutor was in my room. 'Please assemble in the Crystal Room at 7.00 p.m. to meet your fellow delegates' it said.

The Crystal Room was ready to accept us in the latest teaching style. This is an adaptation of the traditional Biblical scene where students used to squat around the feet of an inspired preacher. He usually looks aloft for inspiration and affects a white nightie and long flowing beard.

The leading edge of fashion has changed all this. It is now called a seminar. The scene is set as a horse-shoe of tables with comfortable chairs. The tutors don't rely on gimmicks like polished staffs and threats of eternal damnation any more. They come equipped with the latest in Audio Visual Aids, a combination of controlled lasers with thunder and lightening displays which must be the envy of every Ancient Deity.

Our tutor posed himself on a high stool in the open jaw of tables. This displayed his tooled cowboy boots perfectly.

'Gentlemen' he said 'my name is John Price. I am the Management Development Officer for the Group. I am known as Emdeo. We always know each other by our initials in Head Office. It avoids any confusion caused by names.'

He had a hypnotic Welsh accent. It made you listen to every word he said. Encouraged by an apparently rapt audience, he continued;

'The programme for this week is very comprehensive and thorough. It will demand your every concentration all the time.'

'I will be here all the time to introduce the speakers. They all come from within the Group. This is a seminar. Which means that you will all be expected to take part in it. You will be encouraged to make your views known in the discussion groups ....'

The cadence and lilt of his Welsh vowels seem to dispense with the need to draw breath. I stopped listening to the notes and enjoyed the music.

'....................I will ask you for your reasons. If you can persuade me I will be convinced.'

'Very democratic, we are'.

'Now, gentlemen, we will go round the table and you will all introduce yourselves.'

'Thank you, gentlemen,' chanted Emdeo after the round robin, 'that concludes our business for to-day. Next meeting at 9 a.m. sharp tomorrow.'

He stood to attention in front of his stool. Then he strolled from the Crystal Room with the long, slow stride that is imposed upon all wearers of cowboy boots.

16 delegates drifted to the bar without prompting.

The booze float was established. Quite naturally, the delegates seized the opportunity to talk about Emdeo behind his back.

'Cowboy' said one.

'Head Office creep' said another.

'Dickhead' was suggested.

'Bender'' was mooted.

'Poser' was tried.

'Light-weight wanker.' I suggested.

By general agreement he became El doubya doubya in recognition of his Head Office status.

John Price, Emdeo, El doubya doubya to the delegates, was perched on his stool before we arrived the next day. He looked bright and cheerful. The delegates did not.

'Just to get us started this morning,' he said 'I am going to talk about the Theory of Catering. Then you can all tell me about the practice of Catering.'

'Between us we shall come to know the reality of Catering.'

If it was intended to be a joke it lacked humour.

Too early in the morning for jokes. Too early in the morning for clear thought. Much too early for sharp debate with smart arse tutors. John Price droned away on his lecture like a priest at prayer.

Pleasant waves of nostalgia rolled over me. I dreamed of my favourite things. Like holidays in the sun, Naomi-Naomi Dwight, fast motor cars, Jaysee as a barman in distress, promotion to managing director.

I was formulating an attractive combination of all my favourite things when I noticed the silence.

'Come now, Mr Manager,' said Emdeo petulantly, 'just tell me what your food percentage is .'

'I beg your pardon?' I said. He was talking to me.

Everyone was looking at me.

'I don't want to know your innermost secrets, Mr Manager, just your published results.'
he said nastily.

;57.5%' I said quickly. It sounded like a nice figure.

'There now,' said Emdeo, 'that wasn't so difficult, was it?'

He flipped a switch on his overhead projector. It hissed and glowed like a sullen salamander. He focused the image on a screen.

It was a list of all the Happy Haven Hotels with delegates on the course. Against each
hotel there was a number written in blood red. Mine was 57.5%. The nearest was 59.5%. All the rest were in the lower to mid sixties. Just where the Food percentages were supposed to be.

'The inconsistency of the results shown here,' Emdeo chanted ' is typical of the erratic approach to food control throughout the group. It is said with a great deal of truth' his voice rose higher, 'that the fortunes of hotel groups are made or marred by their food results.'

'Do you realise, gentlemen' he declared passionately, 'that an improvement of just 1% in the food percentage would add another £200,000 to the group's annual profit? '

'And of course,' he added darkly, 'every 1% off the targeted result knocks £200,000 off the group's profit.'

I felt relieved that I had not told him my true percentage. If he felt that way about single percentage points, it would have blown his mind about my result in the lower forties.

I made a mental note to ask the other delegates if they were telling the truth about their food percentages.

After coffee, Emdeo introduced the first guest speaker.

'Mr Victor Benedict here,' he announced 'is known as Veebee. He is the Chief Catering Advisor to the Group. In this capacity he was responsible for setting up and planning many of the operations that you now control. His knowledge of the industry is far-reaching. He had been with Happy Havens for 8 years. He is an examiner for the City and Guilds of London, a Fellow of the Cookery and Food Association, a Member of the Chaine des Rotisseurs .... '

This lengthy psalm of praise went on and on. Mr Veebee, a hairy pink man in a tight fitting blue suit, stood still.

In one huge hand, which seemed to hang unnaturally low by his side, he clutched a battered leather brief case. Knowing his credentials, he looked like a refugee from Gluttony.

Emdeo finally managed to forgo the pleasure of listening to his own voice and left the room.

Veebee elected not to climb onto the vacant high stool. He fell heavily into a chair and revealed tightly laced shoes and regimental sock suspenders.

'Gentlemen,' he said. 'I'm not much of a one for talking in public. That's because I am better at answering questions. So as you have got to ask some questions before I can answer them. I am giving you a questionnaire to complete. Divide yourselves into syndicates of 4 and come back in half an hour.'

Veebee was a man of few words. But you got the impression that when he did speak, he was worth listening to.

The four members of my syndicate read the questionnaire in a conspirator's huddle.

'What we have to decide,' said our most literate member, ' is what we would do if our food percentage dropped by 5 % in one week and 10% the following week.'

'Well what would you do?' he asked.

'Shoot the chef.'

'Crap in my pants.'

'Keep my head below the parapet.'

'What we are required to do,' said the literate one, 'is to make a list of all the things we would do and the order in which we would do them.'

'What we have so far,' I said, 'commit murder, be incontinent and keep our heads down. Any advance on that?'

We discussed the problem at great length. We generated more heat than a haybox. Eventually we had a list of things to do. Not a very long list, but a list none the less.

It was made up of our collective experience in dealing with percentage shortfalls. My contributions was; 'You can tell a great deal about the way a hotel is run by looking in the swill bins.'

A telephone call from Veebee reminded us to go back to the Crystal Room.

'The last syndicate to arrive must have done the most work' he announced, 'so they can be the first to report.'

I had been elected to speak for my group. I had a sheaf of badly written papers to hand. The one on top stated;

'Shoot the chef; crap in my pants; keep your head down.'
'The question under discussion' I began, 'was what we would we do if our food percentage dropped by 5% one week and 10% the following week.'

'We agreed amongst ourselves that this was totally unacceptable to us as managers.'

I paused to test the group reaction so far. There wasn't any.

'Putting to one side the temptation to shoot the chef.'
I paused for laughter which did not come, ' we agreed that the next best thing was to look in the swill bins.'

'You can tell a great deal about the way a hotel is run by looking in the swill bins.'I said. 'what they chuck away is very significant.' I paused for effect. The group registered stony indifference. With an ever mounting sense of isolation, I recited the list of remedies which we had proposed.

Veebee wrote on the blackboard behind him in a delicate script which belied his bulk.

'Is that it?' he asked. When I agreed he said ;

'Thanks.'

A much smoother list followed from another syndicate. Dozens of good ideas came tumbling out, supported by a fan club of participants . The third and fourth groups added many more sound ideas, reflecting long and contentious shades of experience.

Veebee wrote it all into two neat columns on a blackboard. He did not use any of the audio visual aids to enhance his performance.

He drew a broad line from the top to the bottom of the board.

'Why have I done this in two parts?' he asked.

A question on Einsteins Law of Relativity would have been easier.

'Why' repeated Veebee 'have I done this list in two parts?'

You could hear the starter motors grinding. But nobody's engine coughed into life. 'Think about it.' he said. He looked out of the window.

A fraught, taut moment followed. Most of us felt guilty. The question was simple enough. It was just the answer that was hard. The tension mounted with every second that passed. It was like being inside an inflating balloon, waiting for it to burst.

Veebee exhaled heavily. The pressure increased.

'When things go wrong.' he said, 'chef does one half of the list and the manager does the other half.'

The relief felt by the delegates was tangible. It was really quite easy and obvious now that we knew the answer.

'Chef' said Veebee ' cannot be expected to know if the food sales figure for the week is right or wrong. He can check everything that goes over the hotplate. But he cannot check every bill, can he?'

The question was rhetorical. We all shook our heads.

'And many a chef is blamed for a bad percentage when there isn't one. Like when you have a busy week end conference. What happens?'

He scanned the room, seeking inspiration or dumb insolence.

'What happens is'............. there was a hint of passion now ....

'that all the punters are fed with food brought in on Friday and Saturday. And when does the bill go out?' He answered his own question. 'the following week.'
'And I'll tell you something else,' he was warming to his theme of minority group persecuted chefs, 'many is the time that managers come bursting into the kitchens to say "well done, chef " when the percentage is high. But the chef knows it can't be high because he has just had a bad week.'

'So what happens next?'

It was another of those rhetorical questions. We all shook our heads.

'I will tell you what happens. Chef thinks to himself that if the manager can't tell the difference between good and bad weeks, why should he believe any of the results, ever.'

We all tried to look like managers who would never stoop to deceiving chefs.

'I once knew,' said Veebee mournfully, ' a chef who was sacked because he couldn't get his percentages right. It went on and on in the middle and lower fifties for months on end. In the end, the chef and Happy Havens parted company.'

His statement had a cold ring of reality around it.

If that was the punishment for the mid fifties, what on earth would they do to chefs yn the lower forties?

'Several months later,' said Veebee, ' the auditors found out that the comptroller was cooking the books. He robbed the company of several thousand pounds, all of which came from the food sales.'

'But the chef had already gone by then. Nobody said 'sorry' to him.'

Really it was quite a touching story. We all made very proper resolutions about not mis-judging chefs. Shooting them on summary evidence alone was definitely not on. I made a mental note to interrogate Ibrahim, my controller, when I went back to my Happy Haven.

'Most chefs' said Veebee, 'have a strong dislike for figure work. They will duck it if they can."

My chef's problem was even greater than that. At best, he had a nodding acquaintance with the English language. All his calculations were conducted in a series of splutters which sounded like a Hottentot litany. The end result was usually written in ball-point pen on his cuff.

'But the chef must know the cost of every dish in the kitchen. He can't afford not to know.'

'Now you might well say,' -Veebee's narrative style was becoming more attractive with time, like a blind date -'that all the dishes are costed in Head Office and sent out to you as set menus. So what is the point of doing it all again?'

Another expectant pause.

'Because' he said, 'a lot of you don't use the set menus. You make up menus of your own.'

He made it sound like a grave misdemeanour which goes unpunished by default, like farting in church during a service'

'And that is the thin end of a thick wedge. Once you start to skip the costings, it becomes a habit. A bad habit.'

We all tried to look like managers who had no vices at all. 'So after lunch' said Veebee, 'we are all going to do some costings.'

****

"A function organiser," said Veebee, "wants a meal for 250 at lunchtime during the week."

No problem so far. We all love the punters who come for lunch during the week.

'He doesn't want a menu from the Banquet List.' Veebee's earlier strictures about departure from this list were remembered. The popular punter image took a dive.

"He wants; Melon. *Goujon of sole Remoulade*. Roast Leg of lamb with Cranberry Sauce. New potatoes. *Petits pois a la francaise*. Cauliflower *au gratin*. *Pears Belle Helene* or Cheese to follow. Coffee and wines extra. He wrote the menu on the board.

"I want to know," he said "how much you would charge him. What portions you would give him. How much it would cost you. What profit you would make, in pounds and as a percentage."

The delegates sat still, stunned into silence. Sixteen minds in neutral. Sixteen idle minds ticked over, slowly. We looked at Veebee in horror and loathing. The kind of reaction you would have to adult incontinence in a cathedral.

Veebee seemed pleased by the reaction. "Just for starters," he said, "melons cost a pound each. You can get between four and six portions from each one. Go to your syndicate rooms," he said "and you can ask me for any other information you need."

"What the hell is a goujon? How do you make Belle Helene? What's Remoulade? How do you do something *au gratin*? Where can you get Cranberry Sauce?"

"How many legs of lamb do you need for 250?"

"What is *petits pois a la francaise*?"
"How many will have cheese?"
"Why are'nt the menus in English?"

"How about" I said "doing it a little bit at a time?"

"We will need either 42 or 63 melons."

"Should we use English, Welsh, Scottish or New Zealand Lamb?"

"How big is a leg of lamb?"

"If you can get English, Welsh, Scottish or New Zealand lamb, why can't you get Irish lamb?"

"How many gallons of gravy do you need for 250 punters?"

"Why don't we" I said "start at the beginning?"

"You must take out the aitch-bone to carve it properly."

"It would be much better if they had beef or turkey!"

"Why not get a hindquarter of lamb and keep the saddles for later?"

"My mother used to make cranberry sauce."

"Why don't we " I said, "write it all down and start from the beginning."

"Why don't we charge them 25 pound plus VAT?"

"You can get cauliflower in *fleurets*."

"What is a *fleuret*?"

"I dunno. But I've heard about them."

"Why don't we," I said "write it all down and start from the beginning?"

"That's a good idea. Why didn't you say so before?"

"It only just occurred to me," I said.

"Let's take an easy one first," I said "how about the melon?"

"There are several different types of melon. Ogen. *Charentais* and one other."

"What's the other one called?"

"It doesn't matter what it's called. How much does it cost?"

"I think it is water."

"What is?"

"The other sort of melon."

"How much does it cost?"

139

"Veebee said it costs one pound."

"He was talking about the weight, not the cost."

"You don't buy melons by weight. You buy them by the box."

"How many melons are there in a box?"

Nobody knew the answer.

"We can use the one that Veebee said costs a pound. And cut it into six."

"Why not cut it into four?"

"Let's try both" I suggested "and see how much it will cost if we cut it into four or six pieces."

"Anyone got a calculator?"

"You don't need a calculator," said our group genius " to work out the cost of a quarter melon."
"How much is it then?"
"Twenty-five pence." he said.
"And if it is cut into six?"
"That's different," he said "pass me the calculator."

Gradually we got our act together. At first we were like amateur oarsmen on a slave galley, pulling well without real progress. Then we all realised that you get to the same point less painfully if you all pull together.

"Did it really take us three hours to do that?"

"And all we have to show for it is the price of a meal?"

"If it takes four of us three hours to fix the cost of a meal, what about those poor sods in the kitchen?"

"We do not yet know" I said "whether we have got it right. We have to compare our figures with the other syndicates."

We returned to the Crystal Room. Veebee sat at a desk, unmoving and unmoved. He had been in exactly the same position when we left three hours earlier.

Gradually, the noise and hubbub died down.

Veebee rose above the polished surface of his desk like a Nordic sea-god surfacing.

"The best thing to do," said Veebee, "is to write on the board what you think the price should be."

"£33.00 each." I offered.
"£37.00 each
"£38.00 per cover."
"£41.00."

"I think," said Veebee prophetically, "that we had better look at the difference between these prices."

"Let's start with the melon. A nice and easy costing job. At £1.00 each. How many decided to cut it into four?" We all did. "So how much does it cost?"
"25 pence." I said.

141

"Anybody disagree?" One syndicate did. "Why so?" asked Veebee.

"Because we decided that melon by itself is not attractiveenough for a function. So we would cut it into schooners. Decorate it with cherries, ginger and mandarin. Use part of the skin to make a sail and give it better presentation. The price would go up to 35 pence per portion."

"Very good indeed." said Veebee, smiling for the first time since we met.

"*Goujons of sole Remoulade*," said Veebee with the merest hint of passion,

Small fillets of lemon sole, shallow fried in black butter, Served with *Remoulade* sauce, garnished with fried parsley sprig and lemon wedge."

"How much?" Veebee wrote our answers in his neat script on the board. Once again there was a wild swing between top and bottom costs.

"And now to the Roast Leg of Lamb," said Veebee," a much under-rated dish. In Europe and the Latin countries, a festive dish. Like turkey used to be here. Festive lamb was always cooked rare and served with prime vegetables. A special treat for Easter, particularly in Italy. In England we always overcook it. It loses something in the process that mint sauce can't put back." It was the longest statement that Veebee had made so far. He was obviously inspired by food. Perhaps he didn't like people as much. There are no good recipes for people. You are not supposed to cook them.

"How many legs of lamb do you need for 250 covers?"
'23'.'27' '28' '31'

"Anybody got anything to say about this?" Veebee asked innocently.

An intense and scholarly young assistant manager stood up.

"We disagree with the group who would order 23 legs of lamb." That was my group. We had really slaved away to produce that figure. It was precious. As one man, we projected death and destruction rays at the speaker. The recipient was completely unaffected.

"You had better explain that." said Veebee.

Mark Anthony did just that after Caesar's assassination.

"The average leg of lamb," said the scholar, "weighs just over 2 kilos after trimming. The aitch-bone should be removed to make carving easier. We debated the wisdom of having the leg tunnelled out but rejected this as aesthetically undesirable."

I was not really sure what he meant by that. "Roasting in the most economical way would give a shrinkage loss of 20% We would expect to get 8 good portions for every leg. So we would order 31 legs."

143

"23 legs would only provide 180 portions," he added, looking at me.

"I think that is the right number," Veebee said, just like a referee blowing his whistle to calm it down.

"Why?" My syndicate piped in unison.

"Because," said Veebee, "when you carve a leg there is a bone through the middle.

You can't include that in the portion."
My syndicate withered, like adulterers caught in the act.

"So it is always right to reckon on 8 portions per leg and leave plenty of time for chef to carve it."
The rest of menu produced a similar range of discord. Veebee recorded it all on the black board.

"Now let's look at what you would charge for this."
£33.00- £37.00- £38.00- £41.00-

Veebee did not say anything. He looked glum.
He pointed to the smart arse scholarly assistant manager.

"Tell them how you got to £41.00"
Top of the class assistant manager creep stood up. We all loathed him by now.

"Having established our food cost at a realistic level,' he smarmed ' we grossed it up in line with company policy. Then we added a realistic margin for contingencies, presentation and hospitality. We

rounded it off and we kept a bit in hand in order to offer a small discount for prompt payment.
VAT is not included in these figures: it will be shown as an additional payment on the account"

Vebee approved of all that. He gave top marks to the syndicate with the highest price, the best presentation and the flexibility to discount.

At the end of the session, Veebee summarised. "We all learn from these case studies. If it gives you a better knowledge of food controls and functions, it is worthwhile."

"Knowledge", he added sagely, "is never wasted."

I had learned that legs of lamb have bones in them. And that assistant managers have more knowhow than their seniors.

On the last day of the course, John Price, Emdeo, El doublya doubya, summarised.

"Every course sets out to achieve two things. A change of behavior or a change of attitude. Neither of these is measurable so the true value of the course will emerge when you go back to your hotels."

"If, as a result of our discussions, your food results improve, then something of great value has been achieved. It may be that the speakers have taught you something new that you did not know before. Or it may be a chance comment from a colleague which comes as a blinding flash of truth............ ."

He was off on another of his verbal rambles, meandering through the southern slopes of the Orals.

He would be gone for the next half hour. Which left me free to conduct my own course revue. My eyes had been opened during a long drawn out session in syndicate.

We were discussing the finer points of Variance Analysis. It was more boring than watching grass grow. I said;

"Were you all levelling at the start of the course? About your food percentages?"

Affirmative nods all round. But not the really positive nod that makes you believe absolutely.

"But surely there is more to it than that?"

Affirmative nods and negative shakes followed, according to which question was being answered.

"It doesn't figure," I said. "your chefs are no better or worse than mine. Yet you get OK results and I get bollockings."
Raised eyebrows and other manifestations of innocence followed. It didn't need second sight to know that something was not right.

"You bastards!" I said "you are holding out on me."

Then the real teach-in began.

All the greatest inventions are essentially simple.

The wheel replaced the sledge. No one knows who invented it. Then the first scientist invented the axle. Wheels took off. Yet the inventors remain unknown.

Somewhere, at some time, a genius cracked the Happy Haven Food Control System. He, too, was unknown. But his genius lived on. He invented correct food percentages without tears. When my fellow managers told me the simple secret of getting food results right, I was amazed. It was really so easy.

"But surely that is bent?" I said.

"Why?" they said in chorus, "nobody is robbed. The books balance, the banking is correct, the figures tally." It went round and round in my head. Like wheels on axles.

"But what happens,?" I said, "when you are very busy. Won't your food percentage be too high?"

I seemed to have made a very funny joke. When they stopped laughing they told me how to fix that, too.

Emdeo had changed his tone of voice. This implied either a statement of importance or an embryo speech impediment .
"..................................... do not accept that the course ends here. This is but the starting point. When you go back to your hotels you will find that the course notes will help to jog your memory and you will remember what was said and by whom."

"Remember always" he intoned, "one the purer remarks attributed to Confucius. Hear and Forget. See and Remember. Do and Understand."

"Very sound, that one, and very true."

He stood briefly to attention in front of his stool.

"And now gentlemen," he said, "we must say goodbye."
Someone stood up and proposed a vote of thanks for John Price, Emdeo.

Then we all shook hands and went home.
The course was over.

CHAPTER 10 THE TRAP

"You put a mark on every bottle, Martin, every single goddam one?" Naomi was clearly puzzled.

She was dining with me at Louis' restaurant in the country.

She had come back from her European tour and was staying with me for three days. Soon she would be off to Stratford, England, and Edinburgh, Scotland.

"Every single one of them." I confirmed.

"What happens now?"

"I have to check all the bottles in the bar to see if they carry my mark."

"And do they?"

"So far, yes. But I keep hoping."

"Have I got this right? You have to find a bottle in the bar without your mark."

"That's right."

"Then what happens?"

"I keep the bottle as evidence and tell my boss. He will prosecute him."

Naomi thought about it for a while.

"Suppose he is innocent? has that occurred to your and your boss?"

The idea was amusing.

"There ain't no such thing as an innocent barman." I said.

"You know what I think, Martin? Your boss is sick -sick in the head. And he is giving you the same sickness. Has it occurred to either of you that the guy might be innocent? Or that you might both be wrong about him?"

"Honest barmen," I said "are rarer than hen's teeth."
"Some of the nicest people I know work in bars."

"Even the nicest people can be tempted."

"If you treat them as thieves they will behave like thieves."

"Well" I said, "that's the way we operate in Happy Havens. I have to prove to my boss that I can catch him with his fingers in the till and hand him over for punishment."

"Has he got a family? Wife and kids?"

"I think he has both."
There was a long pause. Then Naomi said;

"Are you a heartless bastard, Martin, or do you just pretend to be?"

Her directness shook me. It was an uncomfortable question to answer about myself. Something had been sacrificed to a busy career, but not, I hoped, all feelings.

"Beneath my heartless exterior, sweetheart, is a great big softie."

She looked at me steadfastly for a long time. "I'm glad about that Martin. I really do like you, you are OK. But I get easily hurt by insensitivity."

I could believe that. Someone who worked in Happy Havens Head Office had rejected her. Someone with a small goatee beard had hurt her feelings badly. Someone I had not met on my course last week had hurt her. Someone I would meet one day. Someone I would hurt. Just as he had hurt Naomi.

Very softly, she said; "Mardi will you do something special for me?"

"Of course"

"Go easy on that barman. Believe he is innocent until his guilt is proven. Will you do that for me?"

"Its a deal," I said, "now tell me you are feeling better.

That broad smile lit up her face again. She was her normal self again. Sparkling and twinkling like the galaxy on a clear night, a beacon of enchantment in a sombre world.

And growing in attraction by the minute.

"Sure I feel better Tell me what else you have to do to be the greatest."

"Get my food percentage right." I said.

"Can you do that?"

"I have just been on a course which taught me how to do just that."

In other words, massage the figures until they were right.

"And then you are the best there is?"

"Just one small problem after that, and all is well in my Happy Haven."

"Just one small problem?"

"Yes.I have to find some business to fill in my week-ends. Then my turnover and profits come right. Everybody is happy then and the heat is off."

"Where can you find this business from ?"

"Anywhere I can. The bigger the booking, the happier we all become. The more
We're together, the happier we will be."

"What sort of people stay in hotels for the week end?"

"All sorts of people. Conferences, groups, teach-ins, pray-ins, study groups. Some people just come for a week end to get away from it all and to be quiet."

"What about lovers?"

"We get lots of lovers Darling."

I sent swathes of smiles and positive amorous waves over the table.
She ignored them all.

"What about advertising?"

Reluctantly I brought my mind back to here and now.

"Head Office does all that for me"

"Tell them to try harder."

"Unfortunately, darling, our Head Office doesn't work like that. They tell me what to do."

I wondered if she had made the connection between Happy Havens Head Office and her former lover. On the face of it, it seemed unlikely or she would have said so by now. I wondered if I ought to tell her that the telephone number of her former lover was the same as the telephone number of Happy Havens Head Office. Maybe the subject was still too painful for her to discuss openly. I decided to say nothing further.

"Time to go home"I said, signing Louis' account.

We drove home in silence. I hoped it was contentment after a good meal which caused this unusual silence.

She seemed relaxed enough, driving through a warm night with the hood of my ancient MG down.

When I stopped in the hotel car park I looked at her for a long time.

There was an unspoken question between us. On my part it was a yearning for physical contact and the commitment that goes with it, a desire to be with her and stay with her until the fire that was glowing behind my navel was quenched.

"I am not ashamed of feeling like this,Darling, it is my way of being in love."

"I know" she whispered "Just bear with me a little while longer. I am not ready for this yet, but I will be soon, real soon, Baby."

"Naomi-Naomi Dwight," I said, "you are worth waiting for. Just put me out of my misery as soon as you can, will you?"

"You betcha ass" she replied.

It was impossible to take the matter further. The maiden aunt designers of the MG ensured that when they built a huge transmission tunnel like an unsurmountable wall between the passengers. That wall was definitely not for vaulting tonight.

I walked her to her room and bade her a chaste Goodnight.

****

The following Sunday seemed like many others before it. Just slightly different from weekdays, but not sufficiently so to change the circadian rythm of the average work day.

I sat in my office enjoying a rare moment of uninterrupted silence. It seemed like a good omen. I decided to summarize progress to date -my own personal progress as man and manager. I drew a broad line down the middle of a blank sheet of paper. I think that I learned this technique from Veebee, the cheg. I wrote plus and minus as headings.

After ten minutes of thought, the down side was dominant. Lots of things were just not going my way. Jaysee was still out to get me. Grandaddy Mainframe was supplying the ammunition with relentless regularity. There were still a couple of customer complaints outstanding. I had not earned enough brownie points from my improving food percentages yet to off-set these drawbacks.

And on the up-side? I struggled with that for a while. I had to conclude that it was 'not a lot.'

This worry train of thought was interrupted by the insistent shrill of the telephone.

'Sweetheart; -no mistaking Naomi's voice or enthusiasm- 'have I got something good for you!'

At first I mistook the statement for a question.

'You have?'

'Yes, baby' she said 'and you are gonna be dee-lighted with what I got for you!'

'I am?'

'You most surely are.' She filled the pause that followed, unaware that I was still catching up.

'What would you really like to have if you could choose anything, anything at all?'

Nearly all of the fantasies that I cherished concerned Naomi's body and soul. Somehow it did not seem an appropriate moment to mention it. I knew her well enough by now to recognise that her need to give and share was finely balanced by the need to hold a little something back.

It was not frigidity or self interest that restrained her, of that I was sure. She wanted the act of giving herself to be special, enduring and permanent. She had been bruised by an encounter with someone from Happy Havens Head Office. I wanted her love and commitment. I was prepared to wait patiently until she was ready to trust me implicitly.

'How about a new motor car?'

I detected negative waves down the line. It was plain that my choice did not involve financia; outlay..

'A Royal visit?'

'Uh. uh.' That sounded like another no-no.

'A fairy godmother?'

'Whatever the hell that is, I don't like the sound of it.'

'How about,' I suggested ' a visit from lesser royalty, accompanied by a trainee godmother bringing me a used sports car?'

'Cut the crap,' she said ' ask me what I got for you?'

'Don't keep me in suspense any longer. What have you got for me?'

'How about,' she sang' 45 tourists from Nagasaki, Japan, including four Sumo wrestlers?'

I let out a long, slow whistle. 'When?'

'Now' she replied.

****

I did not need to look at the guest register to know that I could accommodate another 50 sleepers. The house was free for the kind of special week-end events which Jaysee had been snarling at me about. Art Appreciation, Antique teach-ins, Folk Music get togethers, Motor Association Rallies, Catholic pray-ins or any other affinity group gatherings were OK. Parties which offended moral, ethnic, social or political codes were not on.

Not that the house was completely empty. My Happy Haven always attracts a pillow trade of a dozen or so couples who are deeply into thrilling, illicit, sensual cohabitation.

The dirty weekend accounts for a healthy proportion of my Saturday/Sunday sales. It is a mistake to refer to them as sleepers. Their nocturnal activities leave little enough time for rest. During the day time they stand out amongst other guests. They look tired but triumphant.

But I am duly grateful for the steady trickle of undiscounted business which they produce for me.

The dirty weekenders, -we call them huggers, or Smiffs -do not, as a rule, create any problems for us. They are truly low profile punters. They are overtly polite to each other and the staff, helpful and co-operative in all matters of protocol, anxious not to draw attention to themselves. Normal punters just do not behave like that.

Their public behaviour, however, does not reflect their private conduct. Huggers, representing the full gamut of age, colour, creed, social, ethical, professional and gender permutations, can produce some really weird couples.

At Happy Havens, we pass no judgment on huggers. They receive the same treatment as any other punters. The knowledge that their public display of courtesy masks strange and unconventional appetites which can only be unleashed in the privacy of their rooms remains unspoken.

Within the privacy of their rooms, huggers let their libidos fly, unhindered by considerations of delicacy, convention or gravity.

Into the aftermath of their lusty couplings come the room maids. The room maids are unimpressed by the usual debris of lovers, pausing only to wonder, wide-eyed at some of the more bizarre *objets d'amour* abandoned in unlikely places.

When the room is restored to order, the Housekeeper, Iceberg, will inspect it. Iceberg's eagle eye will seek out small disorders quite dispassionately, whether committed by a hyper-active guest or an indifferent room-maid. Only then is she satisfied that the room is fit for human habitation again.

Her endorsement, and Happy Havens stamp of approval, is a thin membrane of quasi silk looped over the loo. By another strange omission, there is no picture of Walter on the loop over the loo.

Occasionally Iceberg is presented with some of the more outrageous by-products of lover's tangles by a puzzled room-maid, Iceberg can classify wierd unknown objects more precisely than a clinical pathologist.

She can distinguish instantly between lost property and the sad detritus of artificially enhanced fornication. Rightful and proper articles such as watches, rings and necklaces, hosiery, corsetage and underwear, trusses, surgical aids and vanitory accessories, false eyelashes, fingernails and dental bridges are sealed into plastic bags to await collection.

Iceberg reserves a special disdain for all varieties of condom with appendages, anything remotely resembling erectile tissue, strokers, stimulators and vibrators.

Her Scottish Presbyterian nature is appalled by pots of potion claiming unbelievable end results, pornographic drawings, photographs and three dimensional models. Such items meet instant destruction in her hands.

But even Iceberg is unable to classify some recovered items. She has concealed, in a very secret place; an odd shaped hot water bottle; a glass eye [blue]; a set of expandable rings in semi-precious metal, too large for fingers, too small for wrists; a malleable golf ball which is suspiciously large; and a medium size unbreakable plastic jar with a siphon pump attached.

Unkind and uninformed gossip amongst the staff suggest that Iceberg's cache of unmentionables is retained for reasons which are vivid but untrue.

CHAPTER 11 SUMO!

I walked to Reception to alert the staff. 45 Japanese tourists, including four Sumo wrestlers and the tour guides were on their way.

Chef was engaging Iceberg in polite but incomprehensible conversation as I approached the Reception counter. Ethel was on duty too. All the people that I needed to tell about the new booking were there.

'Ya, ya,' Chef was talking to Iceberg, 'you haf findings ze oppendown vibrator, no?' 'You get plennigude fox viz ze buzz-buzz oppendown, no?' he added.

He made an explanatory gesture with his right arm which has universal recognition.

'Miss Mcnab,' I said, having de-ciphered chefs message a fraction ahead of her, 'do you think we could accommodate 50 guests here immediately?'

Iceberg, nee McNab, gave me the same frosty look that had failed to quench chefs curiosity.

'My rooms, Mr Hammond, are always ready to receive guests.'

'I wish,' she added gratuitously, 'that the same could be said for the kitchens.'

'Ethel,' I said to the only impartial witness present, 'have we got room for 50 on the same floor for a group of Japanese tourists?'

'Ve haf touristic chaps?'

'Yes, chef. 50 of them. They will be here for lunch.'

'Chaps eat fishes,' said chef, 'plenny fishes and veges and rices. Ve haf plenny zamon, troots, vitebat, harenk, masses and elfisks.'

'Sounds delicious, chef.'

'Viz plenny rices, pellars, fickles, beezers. pinders and .... He struck himself forcibly on the forehead, 'springlox.'

'I expect the menu will be superb, chef. It will be a credit to us all.' Chef set off for his kitchen, muttering explosively as he went.

'Singles or twins?' It was Ethel.

'I beg your pardon?'

'Rooms,' said Ethel, 'for the chaps.'

'Ah, yes,' I said, 'for the Japanese tourists.'

'Singles or twins, then?'

'Some of each.'

'How many do you think it will be, then?'

'I don't know, yet.'

'Then you should know!' It was Iceberg this time.

'Why should he know?' Ethel leapt to my defence.

'Because,' said Iceberg primly, 'he took the booking.'

'I once took a booking,' Ethel replied, 'for two teams of footballers. They booked 30 singles. When they got here, they changed it to 12 twins. They were a bit kinky, though.'

'Not less than four will require singles,' I said, 'with extra big beds.'

'So it is four singles and' .... Ethel counted rapidly, 'twenty three twins?'

'I don't know yet.'

'Then how do you know that only four singles are needed?' It was Iceberg again, sounding a bit miffed.

'Because,' I said, 'four of them are Sumo wrestlers.'

'Four Sumo wrestlers,' said Ethel, giggling.

Iceberg, apparently unmoved by this revelation, said; 'I trust these Sumo wrestling gentlemen don't have the habits of some of the sportsmen who have visited us in the past.'

'All your questions,' I said 'will be answered soon. I can see a coach arriving.'

Naomi was the first through the rotating door. She looked enchanting in her courier's uniform. She wore a hat on one side of her close-cropped hair which seemed to defy gravity and a neat scarf in company colours adorned her neck. My heart began to beat very swiftly at the first sight of her outstretched arms and broad smile.

Our public embrace lasted a fraction longer than decorum would decree as absolutely necessary between business associates. It confirmed for public circulation the rumour that a young American courier who stopped over as my guest quite often was more then just that.

'Where did you find this group, darling, and how did you get them to come here?'

'I was at the airport, you know, Lunnon airport?'

'London, England?'

'When this guy, Ted, you know, Ted the controller, said he had a bundle of tourists from Nagasaki, Japan, who were for Paris, France. They had gotten themselves diverted to Lunnon and needed fixing up for one night before going on to Paris, France, for some kinda exhibition. These Sumos, you know, these really big guys about as big as a Buick are gonna knock the crap outa some other really big guys from Christ knows where ....' She drew a deep breath. ' .... so I said to Ted how about you letting me fix up these guys with a friend whose gotta hotel only thirty miles away and will look after them real good and he really needs the business and will be really pleased about the whole thing, so how about it, huh?'

'But Ted says nuts and he says he can fix them up much closer than that and in any case we got deals with hotels nearer the airport so it don't make no never mind to go wandering off like that.'

'Then how did you manage it, darling?' I said as she took breath.

'Well, this guy Ted, he ain't so bad really. He just likes to appear tough. So I told him he was a motherfuckin sonafabitch and that he really owed me for dozens of favours past. I told him that if he was gonna be a lame-brain needle-dick schmuck all his life he would end up real lonely and everybody would know what a real asshole he was and if they did'nt I would tell them anyway.'

'So what did he do then?'

'He just gives me a Travel Voucher for Happy Havens and says he don't owe me nothin now.'

She shrugged and grimaced. Then she gave me the Voucher which promised to pay for the accomodation and meals for 45 tourists and two staff. My heartbeat accelerated to trip hammer level. Naomi, with her unique brand of persuasion, had just opened up a prestigious new account for the group. It should be worth hundreds of thousands to Happy Havens and I would get the credit for it.

'Darling,' I said, ' I am head over heels in love with the most beautiful woman in the world. I will do anything you ask of me now and forever.more.'

Naomi patted my arm fondly. She said;

'Save it, buster. We got work to do first.'

I looked over Naomi's shoulder. Beyond her a squad of Japanese tourists had lined up neatly in front of the reception counter. 47 in all, including four gigantic man mountain Sumo wrestlers. Plus a small man in a pea green uniform wearing an enormous pea green cap. He was the driver.

'This' said Naomi, 'is Mr Hatsuimoto. He is the group leader. He speaks English.'

I held out my hand in greeting. It nearly touched the top of his head as he bowed low in greeting.

'Bow' Naomi hissed in my ear 'bow from the waist like this.'

We both bowed low in response to Hatsuimoto. Then we all straightened up again.

Naomi said; 'This is Mr Hammond. He is the manager here.'

Hatsuimoto bowed again. So did I. So did Naomi. Before he could move again, I grasped his right hand and shook it.

'You are most welcome here, Sir. On behalf of Happy Haven Hotels it is an honour to welcome you to my country and my hotel.'

Hatsuiomoto bowed again. So did I. So did Naomi.

With surprising swiftness Hatsuimoto turned and directed a stream of non stop Japanese at his group. It seemed to go on for a long time and sounded vaguely menacing. They gave him their undivided attention. It gave me a chance to inspect the group without appearing to be rude.

There were 20 couples, assumedly man and wife. Then four man mountain Sumos, understandably unattached.
The couples were quite small, nearly all wore grey suits. Most wore glasses and cameras which gleamed in the foyer lights.

The Sumos wore dressing gowns, probably the only garment this side of a bell tent which could cover that expanse of flesh. They stood at the back of the group with folded arms and solid scowls.
Apart from an occasional glint of spectacles, the group stood still during Hatsuimoto's harangue. It could not have been a translation of my short speech of welcome. It went on far too long for that. Maybe he was warning his group of the special perils of known social diseases in the civilised West.

Suddenly, like passengers in a braking bus, the group bowed low to me.

They stayed down whilst Hatsuimoto hurled invective at them.

'Bow,' hissed Naomi in my ear, 'Bow you dumb bastard!'

I went down very quickly after that. But I stayed down too long. As I came up, I saw that they were going down again.

We all straightened up for the last time and relaxed.

Then chef appeared and strode towards me purposefully.

Hatsuimoto addressed another fierce harangue at his group. They all bowed to chef. I bowed, Naomi bowed, chef bowed low in response.

'You got' said chef, 'some really big boggers here, ya?'

The registration of guests is a simple process. They give a name, an address and indicate the method of payment. We give them a key swipe, a room card and several hospitable messages designed by marketing.

Ethel was poised to receive guests. Iceberg was poised, clipboard in hand, to suggest rooms. Naomi was close by to observe protocol. Chef was there to assess appetites. I was there to assess the value of the chance business which had just been decanted into my lobby.

Even the driver had risen to the occasion. He was ferrying large suitcases and wicker baskets into the foyer.

'Do you think' said Ethel, 'that they can read English?'

'You don't have to worry about it, Ethel. I have a Travel Voucher for all of them. We will send it to their Head Office for payment.'

'What about registration?'

'We can make a block registration for them later.'

'But how will they know who is in which room?'

'Doesn't matter, Ethel. Mr Hatsuimoto or Naomi Dwight can deal with any messages.'

Then how will they find their rooms? Everything we give them is in a foreign language. Even the numbers are different to theirs.'

'Just give me a moment, Ethel' I said,'I will think of something.'
Iceberg looked at me with contempt. She rolled her eyes to heaven.

'Mr Hatsuinmoto,' I called 'Mr Hatsuimoto, one moment please.'

'I think I've done me back,' said a voice near my elbow, 'I can't stand up straight.

'Mr Hatsuimoto,' I yelled, 'over here please.'

170

'Do you think I could sue your company for industrial injury?' said the voice.

'Mr Hatsuimoto,' I bellowed, 'over here please.'

'How much do you think I would get?' I looked down on the pea green cap of the driver. It seemed a fraction higher.

'You will get,' I said, 'my boot up your arse if you don't shift that bus pronto.'

'Mt Hatsuimoto.' I bowed and he bowed. ' does any of your party understand room and floor numbers?'

'Mr Hammondsan,' he replied gravely, 'all Japanese understand Western characters.'

 With all my heart I hoped that this was true.

'We can,' said Iceberg, 'put them all on the third floor, in adjacent rooms.
'
'There are no singles on the third.' Ethel and Iceberg, in their capacity as Head of Reception and Head of House,had the same debate every day. Honours were about even.

'Then put the wrestling gentlemen into twins.' suggested Iceberg. 'Can't do that.' countered Ethel.

'Why not?'

'Miss Tammond said they got to be in singles.'

It was warming up nicely. It was time for me to intervene.

'Tell you what,' I said to get their collective attention, 'Why not put them all on the third, in adjacent rooms, and put the Sumos into twins? How about that for a good idea?'

Assuming their silence implied total agreement, I turned to MrHatsuimoto.

After the obligatory bow, I said;

'The third floor is allocated to your party, Sir. You can all occupy adjacent rooms.'

'Shall I put Miss Dwight in her usual room?' asked Ethel innocently.

After that it went like clockwork. Hatsuimoto barked a command. A couple stepped forward. Bowed to me, Hatsuimoto, Ethel and Iceberg. Received a key swipe. Found their luggage and headed for the lift. We had a good and steady stream flowing nicely. Apart from one nasty moment when two Sumos got into the lift at the same time, all was well. But even that nasty moment passed off without drama. I uncrossed my fingers and relaxed.

Naomi was on the third floor, showing guests to their rooms. Reception was as smooth as silk, Iceberg and Ethel were too occupied for dissent. The House was ready and willing, chef was beavering away in his kitchen, God was in his heaven and I felt about ten feet tall.

'I can't move me bus.'

The driver of the coach, Daniel, five foot six inches tall including the pea-green cap, was standing behind me.

'Don't bother me now,' I said, 'theres a good chap.'

'But I can't move me bus.' He sounded plaintive.

'And why,' I said in the sure knowledge that I was walking into a trap, 'can't you move your bus?'

'It's stuck.' he said 'stuck under your front porch.'

I was still feeling benevolent when I said;

'Last time we spoke, you had a bad back. What happened to that? You seem to be all right now.'

'It still hurts a lot.' he fondled his spine, 'but it got a bit better.'

'Then let us hope,' I said, watching the smooth flow of guests to the lift, 'that your bus will get better too.'

'But it's stuck,' he said, 'stuck. I can't move it in or out. It's stuck,' he repeated 'under your front porch.'

'Well,' I said, 'I cannot move the porch. I think you should try a bit harder. Just move it to the car park, there's plenty of space there.'

'Cant' be done,' said Daniel, 'it's stuck under your porch......... .'

'Yes, I know,' I said in growing irritation, 'under my porch. You had better show it to me.'

Daniel led the way. Walking fairly spritely for a man with a bad back, I thought.

The porch of my Happy Haven is a fairly functional lump of masonry. It is well lit and spacious enough to allow several vehicles to park whilst their owners check in or make enquiries. It allows coaches and cars to load and unload passengers directly into reception without getting wet in the rain.

Daniel had parked his coach under the porch. Just 'fitted in nicely' he told me.

When the passengers and luggage were unloaded, the bus had risen by about a foot. It was wedged firmly against the roof of the porch. Just as Daniel had said, it was stuck. 'There is,' said Daniel, 'no way it is going to move from under there.'

'Sonafabitch.' I said. It was an expression I had learned from Naomi. Daniel interpreted it as a criticism.'

'It's not my fault me bus is stuck,' he said, 'I didn't do it on purpose. What are you going to do about it? It's company property you know.'

'Why not let the tyres down? That will lower it a bit.'

'Can't be done.'

'Why not?'

'Company policy. Drivers drive busses. Only mechanics are allowed to make adjustments.'

'How about me letting the tyres down? Then you can drive it away.'

'That won't work.'

'Why not?'

'Who is going to pump them up again?'

The thought of Daniel and his bus staying there was not attractive.

'Why not send for a breakdown truck and pull it out?'

'Can't do that' Daniel said flatly.

'Why not?'

'Is'nt brokem down, is it?'

To prove his point, Daniel started the engine. A cloud of black smoke engulfed me. I walked back to the hotel in disgust.

'That bus,' I said firmly, 'has got to be shifted. It is blocking the entrance. Nobody can get in or out whilst it is there. The driver is not very helpful so it is up to us to shift it.'

My remarks were addressed to a think tank of experts who could solve any problem -provided it concerned hotel keeping. Ethel, Iceberg and chef thought long and hard about the stuck coach.

'Call the A.A.?'

'Let the tyres down?'

Chef set off on an excursion of jumbled sentenses, battered grammar and semi-detached syntax, backed by generous gestures.

'You are getting ze really big boggers ..... .' he began. ' .... all oppendown together in ze bom-bom.' he finished.

'Chef' I said, 'that is brilliant. We will do it.'

'Sounds a bit dubious to me.' Iceberg said.

'Better than nothing at all.' Ethel said.

'I need to speak to Mr Hatsuimoto and Naomi Dwight.' I said.

'Iss very gude, ya?' said chef, beaming.

'Mr Hatsuimoto.' I was on the the third floor where all seemed to be quiet and calm. After bowing deeply, I continued; 'it is with much regret that I have to inform you that a practice fire drill will be held soon.'

He looked at me gravely.

'I am sure that you will understand the need to practice efficient, calm evacuation of the building in the event of fire.'

His level stare was unblinking. I continued; 'the time to hold a practice fire drill is with us now.'

His solemn, unmoved mask stared at me, devoid of emotion. 'So I thought it would be a good idea to come and talk to you first about the practice fire drill. Then you could alert your group to what was really happening when the fire bell rings.' This short speech was delivered hopefully.

I smiled and waited for a response.

'Mr Hammondsan,' he said, 'the hotel is on fire?'

'Oh no, no,' I said, 'we are just pretending that the hotel is on fire. It is just a practice fire drill.'

'Mr Hammondsan,' he said 'you are pretending to set your hotel on fire?'

'Please understand me, Mr Hatsuimoto,' I was pleading now, 'the hotel is not on fire and I will not set it on fire.'

'Ah so. The hotel is not burning!'

'No, it is not burning. But when the bell rings, you must all pretend that it is on fire.,

'You will ring a bell' he said, 'and then you will set the hotel on fire?'

'No, no. I won't set the hotel on fire. But I will ring the fire-bell. When I ring the fire-bell, you must all leave the hotel.'

'Ah so, all Japanese must leave the hotel?' He bowed very low.

'Mr Hatsuimoto'. I leaned forward and addressed his shoes. 'I do not want you to leave the hotel -only for a short time after the bell sounds. Then you can all come back.' We both stood up again. Hatsuimoto waited for me to say something. I took a deep breath.

'The bell will sound. Ding-dong. You scram. Plenty quick, O.K.? All come back.Chop chop, O.K.'

'O.K.' he said, 'Ding dong. Scram, all out. All come back, plenty quick O.K.'

'Mr Hatsuimoto,' I said 'you are a treasure!'

There is a strange excitement involved in fire alarms. I pushed the 'TEST' button with Iceberg and Ethel as witnesses. All over the hotel in every nook and cranny an urgent shrillness sounded. The emergency lights came on, a strident summons to leave the building at once was beamed at everyone, even the deafest mute must have known of the emergency status.

Based upon the assumption that nothing ever catches fire on the Lord's Day my punters were unmoved by the clamour. A Hugger rang up to enquire of the hotel was on fire. He was assured that it was not.

'That's all right, then.' he said.

Two unreserved guests arrived at reception. 'Do you have any vacancies? Is the hotel on fire?'

He was told yes and no. 'That's all right then.' he said.

The Bars Manager presented himself to reception.

'Closed the bar,' he said cheerfully, 'got the takings in my pocket. Left the float behind.'

A party of six strolled through the front hall.

'Thought we would have some lunch here, have you got a menu?' He had to bellow to be heard above the din.

'We will wait in the bar.' he added.

The Japanese group's arrival in the front hall was announced by a piercing whistle, even louder than the alarm bells.

Like a crack football team with attendant coach, they trotted down the main stairwell in pairs, in perfect step and harmony. They were urged along by Hatsuimoto who carried a whistle set firmly in his teeth.

90 legs in unison, including eight Sumo wrestler legs which moved with surprising grace and speed,

descended the stairs under perfect control. At the bottom of the stairs they bore right like a centipede on a twig and headed for the wide open front door.

Their direction was already set. Iceberg, Ethel, chef and I bordered the lane to the front door.

Daniel and Naomi stood either side of the bus door. Hatsuimoto urged them into single file to board the bus at a constant and cracking pace.

When they were all in the door shut with a hydraulic hiss. A cloud of black smoke erupted from the exhaust. The coach slid slowly towards the car park.

Four Sumo wrestlers glowered balefully from the back seat. They were wholly unaffected by the jubilation and applause of Iceberg, Ethel, chef and I. Even Daniel the driver was grinning as his coach slipped from under the front porch.

CHAPTER 12 THE T.S.O.

Monday morning had to be an anti-climax after that Sunday. I had waved goodbye to my Japanese tourists early in the morning. Naomi had insisted on it .She had tipped me out of bed very early in the morning.

I had wanted to linger and relax after a night of unconsummated passion which left me drained of energy. It left Naomi bloody but unbowed, her pleas in mitigation uttered softly but firmly in defence of an emotional barrier that had still to crumble.

Naomi had departed with the Japanese party. She promised to ring me from Paris, France the moment that she arrived.

I sat in my office and contemplated two firsts. It was difficult to place them in ranking order. Naomi would come back soon and I could look forward to that reunion with profound yearning and growing confidence.

The other first was the dramatic change in my management fortune. From a position at the bottom of the Happy Haven Hotel pecking order in Jaysee's patch, 'with the all-time record low food percentage' I had risen to the anonymous middle rank. I was no longer singled out by Grandaddy Mainframe as the whipping boy of the group.

That honour had been conferred upon some other unfortunate manager.

Admittedly, this dramatic change had been achieved by massaging the figures to suit the need rather than the facts. My fellow managers on the course had assured me that it was common practice throughout the group.

Ibrahim, my Pakistani comptroller had grave doubts about it when I explained it all to him but he had given in eventually. Now my Happy Haven was a model of excellence on paper.

The other cause of so much distress to my District Manager, the low level of week-end business, had just been rectified in a most dramatic way.

Happy Haven Hotels now had a prestigious new account with a major tour group, thanks to the skilful negotiations conducted by .... Martin Hammond, assisted by Naomi-Naomi Dwight.

It sounded better that way, and if it figured in my management bonus, I would be sure to show my appreciation to Naomi.

And I was getting even closer to my main quarry, the Bars Manager.

'You catch him, Hammond, I will prosecute him' Jaysee had snarled at me a long time ago.

Fortunately, Jaysee had left me alone since our last vitriolic meeting and I seemed to have faded into a kind of limbo.

Either his attention was distracted elsewhere or he was impressed by my improved performance.

All in all, I could congratulate myself upon a splendid performance. I could look forward to the warm approval of my colleagues and masters, maybe even a small promotion might be in order? I might even be promoted to Head Office and become known by my initials instead of name. Emaitch, perhaps?

....
'ead 'office on the line for you, Miss Tammond.'

'Thank you Ethel. Put them through, please.'

'Good Morning,' I boomed, 'Emaitch here.'

'I would like to speak to Mr Hammond, please.' The voice was junior female.

'This is Martin Hammond.' I said crossly.

'Oh, Mr Hammond, I'm so sorry. I thought you said some other name.. just one moment, I'll put you through.'

I stuck my tongue into the mouth piece. After a long pause and a repeat of the identity crisis, I heard;

'John Price, Emedeo here,' he said' I am speaking to Martin Hammond, am I not?'

Two can play at that game, so I said;

'Just one moment, John, I have someone on the other line.'

'Then ring me back when you are free.' he snapped.

I let an hour go by. Then I called him.

‚Ah yes,' he said 'Martin Hammond.' He made it sound like something they sing at Cardiff Arms Park during the Rugby finals.

'Not so busy now, are we?'

'What is it,' I said 'that I can do for you?'

'When we attended a course on Food and Beverage Control a month age, Martin' he chanted, 'the very last thing that we all did was to agree to submit a post course report containing constructive comments on the areas in which the course could be improved for the benefit of all those who would follow on.

Most of us have replied by now, but some of us have not. Martin Hammond is on the list of those who who have not done so. We ask ourselves why this is so?'

'Because I forgot' I said. I was tempted to say 'we forgot' but prudence forbade it.

'Then there is a strong possibility that the same oversight applies to our post-course project, isn't there?'

'Er, yes.' I said, wondering what post-course project he meant. Certainly the post-course project to remedy the food result figures had been successful. But I knew that he was not thinking of that.

'Because we all promised faithfully when we were on courses that when we went back to our hotels we would prepare a project on the course subject and let our Emdeo have a sight of it in order to assess what course would be suitable as a follow-up, didn't we?'

I could vaguely recall such heady promises made a long time ago.

'The project,' I announced, 'is in hand.'

'Then, Mr Manager' said Emdeo, 'I can look forward to hearing from on two different themes. When will these dates be?'

'Very soon,' I said 'very soon.'

Emdeo sighed heavily. 'Very soon, Mr Manager, is not a definite date. You must be much more precise than that. Without a definite date, you cannot have a definite objective. Without a definite objective, you do not know in which direction to aim. It is most important that you lay down certain times when this report and project will be finished.'

He was starting to make a speech. The flood gates were opening slowly and the resonant Welsh vowels were beginning to flow through. Some action was called for to stop the flow.

185

'The course report' I said, 'will be with you within a week. The project will be complete by the end of the month.'

'Very good, Mr Manager,' Emdeo chanted, 'very good. I am entering the dates on your file and I will expect to hear from you by then.'

He rang off.

I turned my attention to more pressing matters like today's business. My mail contained a bluff official envelope which I put to the bottom of the pile. I dealt with the more pleasant aspects of running a hotel which involves taking money from punters.

Then I frowned at the less pleasant aspect of running a hotel which involves parting with the bread taken from the punters.

Finally I opened the bluff, official envelope which was addressed to Jaysee and I, the joint licensees of the hotel.

It was from the Trading Standards Officer, a civil servant dedicated to the proposition that the Great BrItish Public shall not be swindled, except by common consent and politicians.

The contents were far from routine. In fact, the dry official prose made me sit bolt upright in my chair and emit a long, slow, tuneless whistle.

A Trading Standards Officer, known as a TSO to all, had visited, unannounced, and ordered a whisky from the bar. The date, time and place was confirmed by the complaining TSO.

The official complaint confirmed that the measure dispensed was correct but stated that the spirit was not of the alcohol proof printed on the label. In other words, the whisky was watered. In recognition of this serious transgression, the joint holders of the liquor license, Jaysee and I, were to be prosecuted.

It meant that the Bars Manager had just slipped into my gaff net after a long and eventful vigil. I began to plan the confrontation with the Bars Manager that would follow very soon. I could not resist a smug smile of satisfaction.

'You catch him, Hammond, I'll prosecute him' Jaysee had snarled at me during our last meeting.

And now I could hand him over, trussed and neatly tied up, caught bang to rights in a trap of exquisite irony.

Indirectly, he had been trapped by my vigilance and now the net had closed around him. Although I could congratulate myself on the capture, it was not the cleanest of shots which had got him in the end. It was really a ricochet of alarming complexity which brought about his downfall.

Before Jaysee and I could prove our innocence in court he would have to be prosecuted. The evidence was there, in the brown, official envelope.

Confronted by the evidence, which he read very slowly and thoroughly, the Bars Manager wriggled and squirmed like live bait. I put aside all other considerations in pursuit of the facts.

'How', I asked 'did the water get into the whisky?'

'No idea at all.'

'Any suggestions which might be helpful?'

'None' he replied.

'Let's try another tack' I suggested. 'According to the roster, you were on duty during both shifts on the day it happened and the day after.'

'I don't deny it. So were a lot of other people.'

'But it does mean' I said 'that you were there in the bar when it happened.'

'When what happened?'

'When the TSO bought a tot of baptised whisky.'

'Did he say that it was me who sold it to him?'

'No he didn't.'

'Then it is his word against mine, isn't it?'

'Who else could it have been, then?'

'Don't know.'

I smiled at him in what I hoped was a sinister way.

'Who else could it have been? ' I made a pretense of looking at the roster.

'Jean was also on duty that evening.' He said it reluctantly.

Jean was the relief barmaid who helped out when others were off duty. The slackest time was at week-ends. Jean worked every week-end.

'Are you saying that it was Jean, then?'

'No, I am not saying that.' he replied.

'Then, by a process of elimination, we can agree that it was Jean or you?'

'Yes' He said, wincing..

'Well done,' I said, 'at least we are in agreement about something.'

I remembered Jaysee saying that to me. The impact was devastating.

He remained silent.

'So' I said after a long pause 'we now know that either Jean or you served watered whisky that evening?'

He nodded and shrugged at the same time. He fell silent, looking down.

'Where,' I asked 'did the whisky come from?'

'A bottle.'

'What sort of bottle?'

'A glass one' he replied.

I suppressed a strong desire to punch him on the end of his nose. I forced a smile instead.

'What size of bottle?'

'You tell me the brand' he said 'I'll tell you the size.

'House brand' I said. 'You do know the house brand, don't you?' He nodded.

It was called Bonnie Prince. It was specially blended for Happy Havens by the distillers.

'So which bottle would that be in?' I asked.

'A tregnum'.

'And that would be on optic?' He nodded again.

'Describe it.'

'Triple bottle size, upsidedown with a glass optic.' He was still looking down and his voice was barely audible.

'Very good' I said' now tell me how water can get into a glass bottle mounted upside down with a leak-proof optic as the only way out?'

'I don't know.'

'Then I'll tell you.' I said. 'The only way in for water is through the neck.'

He looked at me for the first time. He had all the hallmarks of a frightened man.

I fought back all the feelings of pity that welled up inside. Instead I remembered the many hours of discussion that had followed a series of bad stock reports in the past. I had shown pity then, but my district manager had been quite positive about the Bars Manager.

'I've seen straighter cork-screws' had been his verdict and I had taken all the blame so far.

'What we have to establish,' I said 'is who poured water down the neck of that bottle.'

'Are you accusing me?'

'At the moment,' I said, 'we have established that either Jean or you served watered whisky to a TSO. We have also agreed that the water got in by the neck of the bottle before the optic was fitted.'

'But you think it was me that put the water in?'

'Was it?'

'No' he said 'it wasn't me.'

'Any idea who it could be then?'

'None at all.' he replied 'far too many people have access to the bar. It could be anyone of them.'

'How come?' I asked. 'You or whoever is in charge locks the bar when the session is finished and hands in the keys to Reception.'

'Well' he said 'someone goes into the bar after each session. I know because lots of little things are moved very slightly.'

He looked at me pointedly. He must have known that I was checking his stock for brought in bottles. Maybe that was why I had been unable to catch him, although it was a mystery how he knew.

'Even if that were so,' I said cagily' no-one has anything to gain by adding water to the whisky.'

'Not unless they wanted to set me up.'

'Now why,' I asked 'would anyone want to do a thing like that?'

'If I knew the answer to that' he said, 'I wouldn't be here now trying to explain how the water got into the whisky.'

'What we have to ask ourselves here,' I said with fingers steepled, 'is who stands to gain from selling watered whisky.'

He took a long time to think about his answer to that one.

'The house gains most,' he said 'because it is selling less whisky for the full price.'

I nodded in agreement. We had discussed the fine tuning of bars results many times before. It would have been unwise for him to come up with any other answer.

'So you would expect a surplus on the stock report, wouldn't you?'

'Yes.'

'But there is no surplus,' I said, playing my trump card. ' in fact there is a deficit. Do you want to see the stock report which proves it?'

He shook his head slowly. He looked weary and pale.

'So' I continued relentlessly, 'if there is no surplus on the report it means that someone must have taken cash from the till instead.'

'Or else it means that there is a stock error.' he said.

'Every time that I receive a stock report here you tell me that there is a stock error. I am fed up with hearing that line from you. You have used it too often. I just don't buy it any more.'

'Do you want me to leave?'

I just managed to control my jubilation. Jaysee's gypsy warning rang in my ears.'They should always resign, Hammond' he had said, 'never sack them.'

'Do you want to resign?' I countered.

'Yes' he said 'right away. I wont stay here and be accused of stealing. I'll go somewhere else where I will be trusted.'

'Good day to you' I said, 'our business together is finished.'

CHAPTER 13 AFTER THE BALL WAS OVER

A full month went by without any reaction from Head Office. Even Jaysee kept silent. In fact, the only remarkable thing was the absence of any comment or acknowledgement of the significant improvement in the performance of my Happy Haven. All the cost and profit margins had been achieved to the satisfaction of Casino Chips, who registered grudging approval instead of strident electronic angst. A new Bars Manager had been appointed for a trial period of three months.

I began to feel a bit miffed about being ignored.

'After all,' I complained to Naomi over dinner one evening, 'you would think that a pat on the back wouldn't be so difficult to hand out, considering the achievement. I mean, catching a crooked Bars Manager and introducing the entire Japanese nation to the heady delights of Outer London whilst getting the profit margins right would at least merit a mention in despatches wouldn't you?'

'Relax,' she replied, 'give it time.'

'It is not as though they don't know where to find me', I said,

'I get dozens of stupid requests every day from Head Office. I was asked to fill in a form from Accounts which asked me if I knew how to work

195

out percentages. And another from Training which gave me a choice of three courses to go on.'

'Relax,' she said, 'let your balls hang out.'

'I am beginning to think that I am in the wrong job'

'Mardy' said Naomi earnestly 'if you think you are in the wrong job you should just quit. You can get a better job than the one you have with your qualifications and experience.'

'Unfortunately, sweetheart. it is not as simple as that. If I just quit and walk away from it, sure, I can get another job with another hotel group. But it will not be very different from the job I have now. , All the groups operate in much the same way so no great advantage comes from just changing the job for it's own sake.'

'The slight differences that do exist between the hotel groups are not influenced by the managers. If someone just turns up to change the carpets or paint the place in a different colour, it is not because the manager requested it.'

'I don't even set the menus or the wines list, it is all done for me. I, and hundreds like me are not really managers in the true sense of the word-we are just spear chuckers who obey orders.'

'But why do you have to take all that crap from District Managers then?'

'Nobody has given me a good answer to that yet'

We turned our attention to the food being served by Louis.

'Does it have to be with a group?' Naomi asked 'surely they don't own all the hotels?

'The groups own about one half of all the hotels. But that half contains more than a third of all the rooms and nearly all of the biggest and best hotels around. The groups are expanding and they are in a strong position to acquire any hotels which do come on the market.'

'So what it adds up to' I said 'is that if you wan't a career and promotion, you must be part of a group and get promoted.'

'And is that what you wan't, Babe?'

Naomi was serious and the question was disconcerting.

'Yes, I do' I said after a long pause.' and to make matters worse, I seem to have got off to a bad start with Happy Havens'.

'Babe' Naomi said 'you will make it O.K.' You are an achiever. I know you have got it in you and you will get there.'

'Believe me' she added 'One day it will work out for you. I just know it will.'

I wish my District Manager shared your good opinion of me. He said I was a wanker- a lightweight wanker.'

Naomi studied me for a long moment.

'You could prove him wrong, Babe.'

'How could I do that?.' I asked.

'By fixing everything that he says is wrong - even if it is'nt.'

'Do you think I could do that?.'

'Do you believe in yourself?'

'Yes' I said 'I could be the best there is.'

'Then go to it, Babe,' she said 'go to it and win!'

The cloud of depression that had settled over me began to brighten a little.

'I will show him,' I said 'just what a light weight wanker can do.'

'Ataboy, said Naomi.'you just hang in there, Babe,you can do it!.'

'Darling Muse Naomi' I said, 'I feel better already.'

'Let's celebrate tonight. Let's get smashed and drink to the downfall of my enemies.'

Naomi was smiling again. That broad smile which lit up her face and radiated warmth.

'A lot of things you are Babe,' she said 'but a wanker you ain't. If you wanna celebrate, I just got a great ides.'

'You have?.'

'Sure thing.'

She had slipped off her shoes under the table and her stockinged big toe was rubbing hypnotically up and down my leg as she said softly:

'Why drink and drive when you can smoke and fly, Babe?.'

The suggestion, the stockinged big toe and the smile combined to convince me.

An electric thrill was glowing just behind my navel and it spread slowly down to all those parts where the sun don't shine as I sped back to the hotel.

****

'What I have here,' Naomi said, 'is an Amsterdam Special. Ready rolled with built in roach and all the best bits of Afghani Black in a great mix. Guaranteed to fly you to the moon and back again.'

It seemed like an appropriate time to listen to Dire Straits so I set it up for extended play.

The music flowed, soothed and slowly, very slowly, the uptight tensions injected by Happy Havens leeched away from my muscles and insides. My mind relaxed, easing and unwinding the tourniquet which bound me to duty, responsibility and society.

Naomi was unbuttoning my shirt with slow deliberate ease when she said:

'Honey, just relax a little, willya. Let your balls hang out.'

She has slipped out of her dress and led me gently back to the long settee. Her clothes were scattered untidily on the carpet and my shirt, tie and pants joined them. A few adroit tugs from Naomi soon parted me from any remaining gear and we sprawled back on the scatter cushions.

Naomi smoothed and whispered away the few token tensions that remained.

'Relax, Babe, just relax.' and

'Stay calm, Honey, deep down calm'. and

'Take it easy, Sweetheart, easy, easy now.'

And for one thrilling moment she buried my face in her boobs just as Dire Straits zoomed through a long, rooting phase, misnamed as Brothers in Arms.

She lit the joint - 'Angels Breat' she called it and drew on it deeply before passing it to me.

'Really, really good.' I said, feeling the narcotic kick-start the pysche, 'best I ever had.'

Naomi drew heavily on the joint again, held the smoke in her mouth and exhaled a long aromatic cloud.

'Babe' she said 'I can fly'

She handed the magic wand to me.

I inhaled a long draught and for one panic moment I fell, tumbling through depths, accelerating into a void, fleeting through empty deeps, spinning slowly into an abyss.

But the fall checked, levelled out and I rose again. Gently at first then I soared upwards swiftly into fleecy white clouds and a wide blue yonder.

I turned and twisted under total control. I could glide or dive at will, totally at ease in all dimensions of time and space, a joyous celebration of full freedom to roam at will.

We drew again, in turn. Our worlds blurred and bloomed, fried and froze, grew large and diminished again through bright lights and clarion echos of spirals, whorls, shapes, patterns, rainbows, ever moving, never still, but always beautiful, calm and benevolent.

Nothing jars in Paradise, everything sings in harmony, the welcome holds and embraces you.

Flowers everywhere, sunshine, dappled glades and peaceful, slow shallow swoops from branch to branch of Joy to Pleasure.

I focused from a cloud to a trail of tiny blue flowers, admiring their perfect symmetry amidst a leafy cluster.

I came to a ribbon, tied in a bow, concealing a clasp. It did not seem to belong there, so I tweaked it apart, very, very gently.

'I've undone the Gordian knot' I said in triumph as Naomi's last scrap of underwear floated away like a butterfly.

'It just came away in my hand and I think it is just beautiful and I will wear it on my head for ever.'

'On your back' said Naomi, 'there is a small spot, sorta pink, and when you move it moves. Not a big move, Mardy, but a cute little tremble over a rib and back again, like it can't settle down. Will you make it do it again?.'

'I am very interested in your right knee,' I said 'but I can't remember why'.

'Just pop up,' Naomi said, 'and ask the angels. They know everything.'

'What a good idea' I said, 'shan't be gone long.'

'When you get there,' Naomi said, 'ask for Gabriel. He's the most helpful one. Plays the trumpet real good' she added.

One quick puff and I soared off on my errand with every nerve-end tingling, intent and purposefully content in a living dream on leave from reality.

Most of the people that I met on the way were either euphoric or cheerful happily engaged in their own pursuits, contemplating trivia with gravity or staring at space with awe.

But a round orange face with eyes screwed up in ecstasy pointed a round black finger at me and said:

'Why do you wear your heart on your sleeve, silly man?.'

'Because' I said, 'because...............'

I fumbled around even more for an answer to a very hard question.

'Because, I don't know where my heart should be.' I blurted out.

Orange face laughed and laughed for a long time as I fell back down again, whilst pointing a spade black finger at my throbbing heart.

I fell gently at first, then at increasing speed like a sycamore leaf tumbling and twisting down to earth on an Autumn day.

The earth was dark, warm and cosy and swayed hypnotically when I got there, scared and trembling after the fall.

Naomi-Naomi Dwight from....I could'nt remember where was holding me very tight and rocking me slowly from side to side and crooning softly.

'Relax, Babe, relax. Just take it easy...hang in there Honey. Easy, easy now, softly, softly, precious, hang in there, Mardy, I got you, you are safe and

O.K. now Babe, just relax a little bit more, just relax and'..............'

I think we were both crying out loud when we drifted off into the velvet darkness that is sleep.

Waking up after smoking joints brings a feeling of well-being and benevolence unmarred by the lethargy, torpor and dehydration associated with alcohol. It felt already like the beginning of one of the better days. I was glowing quite cheerfully, ruminating amongst the more pleasant of the previous evening travelogue as Naomi appeared from the kitchenette.

She was wearing my dressing gown as she carried a tray with coffee and fruit juice, cups and glasses.

'I grow very fond,' I said 'of women who get up early in the morning to bring me my breakfast in bed'

'Cream and sugar?' she said.'

'It shows that they have a high regard for the continuing creature comfort of their menfolk.'

'Orange or Grapefruit?' she replied.

'The kind of woman that I like more than any other woman in the whole world would be the one who not only got up to serve my breakfast in bed but shortly afterwards got back into bed to engage in what we Brits rather endearingly call Hanky Panky.'

'Shadupp' said Naomi 'and eat your breakfast. Yours is the coffee and cream and Orange Juice.'

We drank in silence for a while whilst I beamed positive seduction waves at her.

'I know exactly' said Naomi 'what you Brits mean by Hanky Panky.'

'You do?.'

'Uh-huh.' It sounded pleasantly positive this time.

'And?'

'My mamma told me it was O.K.'

'She did? What an enlightened mother you have sweetheart.'

Naomi looked at me for a long moment, weighing, assessing, measuring critically like an angler with a specimen catch.

'My mamma said it was O.K. provided it was for purposes of procreation only, in the Missionary position and even then she said you mustn't ever smile.'

But she did smile. In fact she laughed out loud and got the giggles several times. And when all this happened, she wasn't in the Missionary position either.

CHAPTER 14 THE WRECKING CREW

But in spite of my impatience, or maybe because of my impatience the daily deliveries from Head Office remained depressingly mundane.

A boring summary from Accounts pointed out that I did not know how to work out percentages correctly and a memo from Marketing told me how to sell hotel services by telephone.

Then, unannounced, the Wrecking Crew came down like the wolf on the fold.

My office is fairly small. if you felt inclined to do so, you could probably swing a small cat in it. There is enough room for one person to sit on either side of a modest desk in relative comfort.

With four standing and one sitting, it becomes constrained and uncomfortable. The Wrecking Crew, I had yet to discovered, rarely sit down. They prefer to remain standing .

'Let me introduce my team, Mr Hammond' said the only one who smiled.

'I am Liaison. From Special Projects.'

'I'm Food and Bev.'

'I'm Marketing.'

'I'm Control.'

They sounded off like soldiers on parade.

'Hullo,' I said, 'how long are you staying?' Not my usual welcome speech.

'That depends,' said liaison.

'On what?'

'On how much co-operation we get from you.'

'What do you mean by co-operation?'

'Able and willing assistance, freely given without reservation.'

His smile remain fixed as he spoke. But his eyes did not smile. He managed to convey hostility within the soft spoken word, just hinting at the iron fist which was concealed.

'Where are you staying?' I asked, matching his hostility, 'we are fully booked here, you know.'

'We have confirmed reservations here.' liaison was still smiling. The smile of a man who is very sure of himself. like a chess champion whose opening moves are swift and positive, worked out in advance.

'When will you start working?' I asked.

'Our assigmnent has already begun.' he replied.

'How come?'

'When we went to our rooms, we were able to complete an S.R.I.'

'S.R.I.?' I asked, 'just what is that?'

'Standard Room Inventory' he said cheerfully 'as in your Operations Manual.'

I could feel my temper rising, more from frustration than insult.

'I see' I said 'and was it all right?'

'Absolutely perfect' he replied.

For some strange reason this sparked off a reaction amongst the others. They all grinned. Mirth without humour.

'And just what are you doing now?' I asked 'a Standard Management Inventory?'

'Good Heavens me no, dear boy' said Liaison, 'we always call upon the manager when we are on the premises. As a matter of courtesy.'

He shook his head slowly as he spoke. The *bonhomie* remained, but his eyes were stony and unblinking.

Suddenly he came across like one of those cultured, sadistic pervs who terrify small boys. I suppressed a shudder. I could think of nothing further to say.

'We will all meet again here in the morning,' he said, 'shall we say 8'o' clock?'

They filed out of my office. Four men dressed in light grey suits. Wearing dark blue ties with a Walter motif. Carrying identical brief cases. They left the door open and an intimation of suave hostility stayed behind.

Ironically, it seemed that Head Office had responded to me at last. By keeping a deliberate silence for a month to soften up the nerves and then sending in the shock troops unannounced.

It seemed that the old argument with Jaysee had not been forgotten after all, just put to one side whilst waiting for the right moment to arrive. Which was right now.

****

'Did you have a late night?' asked Liaison.

'No more so than usual' I replied, recalling a particularly fractious overbooking that I had been called out to deal with during the night.

'I didn't wait for you this morning' said Liaison 'I wanted to get the chaps started.'

'O.K.' I said 'where are they?'

'Food and Bev has gone to the kitchen. Control is working in the Front Office. Marketing is working on the Sales and forward bookings.'

'And what about you?'

The merest flash of quick anger was covered by a broad smile.

'I thought that you and I might spend a little time getting to know each other.'

'What do you want to know?'

I was feeling tired and edgy. Somehow, I seemed to have lost the initiative.

I felt sure that I was being manipulated by Liaison. I did not know how to deal with his ingratiating manner and he was definitely getting to me.

I had made several frantic telephone calls to other managers in the group last night. I had put the same question to all of them; 'How do you deal with the Wrecking Crew.?'

The advice that I received ranged from;

'Just pretend that they are not there' to 'Have your resignation ready -they don't take any prisoners.'

Naomi's advice from Madrid, Spain, seemed like the best; 'Just hang in there, baby,' she had said.

'What do you wan't to know about me-from the moment of conception or from the moment of birth?' I asked Liaison.

'Let's just take it from the moment you became manager here.' he said. He was still beaming goodwill when he added;

'And if you give me any more of that crap, Sunshine, I will suspend you from employment on the spot and you will not be re-instated at the very earliest before I have completed my report, which will be, as a conservative estimate, the other side of Christmas. Even then, re-instatement would be a possibility rather than a probability.'

When you come up against that degree of clout, it is best to bow before it.

'From the moment that I became manager here,' I said, 'that would be a good starting point?'

'Yes' he said jovially, 'that's the spirit.'

'Do you think' he said as I was arranging my mind into the required order, 'that we could have some coffee sent in?'

'Yes of course' I said, rather too quickly.

'Splendid' he replied' perfectly splendid.'

CHAPTER 15 THE ASSIGNMENT

'At the end of every assignment,' said Liaison 'we have a few words with the unit manager.'

Like a pre-planned journey, the assignment had come to an end by 4.30 p.m. the following Friday.

The Wrecking Crew had been in my Happy Haven for 10 days, but, like all Head Office staff, they did not work during the week-end.

The same privilege was not open to resident managers and staff. We needed the slack time on Saturday and Sunday to compensate for the slowing up caused by the strident presence of the Wrecking Crew between Monday and Friday. Their interrogation of all the Heads of Department had ruffled many feathers. I had spent long hours with Iceberg, Chef, Ethel and the Restaurant Manager, soothing away their fears and antagonism.

'They won't be here for long,' I had said on many occasions, 'they are just doing their job.'

'They waste so much of my time' sighed Iceberg,'just counting sheets and pillow cases. Surely such senior executives don't have to do that?'

'Zis Food an Bev bogger,' said chef, 'I do not truss. He iss too long in ze larder.'

'That one called Control,' said Ethel 'I think he is a pervert. Every time I turn round he is looking over my shoulder. Makes me shudder.'

'Every time they have meals,' said the Restaurant Manager, 'they write about it. Fill in big reports about every thing they eat. Never drink anything, though.'

'It will soon be over,' I reassured them all, 'they have other fish to fry elsewhere. Just be patient a little while longer.'

And now the Wrecking Crew were lined up in front of my desk, standing still.

Liaison, Marketing, Food and Bev and Control.

'You realise, of course,' said Liaison 'that what we are about to tell you isn't the full and complete version of our findings. That report is reserved for the Executive and will be written up in due course. When it is complete, you will receive a copy.'

'Nonetheless,' he continued 'there are several matters which must be brought to your attention as unit manager. All stand in need of immediate action.'

His voice had the timbre of a judge passing sentence. A man who has heard both defence and prosecution arguments and believed neither.

'My verbal report' he said 'will refer to each department in turn.'

'And I will be most pleased' he added 'if I can proceed without interruption.'

The last remark was directed at me. We had crossed swords on many occasions during the past two weeks.

He liked to ask the same question at least twice, but always worded in a slightly different way. When I pointed this out to him he had replied;

'I am always interested in your answers.'

'And that is your justification for asking the same question over and over again?'

To which he had replied;

'It is the difference between your replies which interest me most.'

'Vive la difference.' I countered.

'Not when the difference amounts to several thousands of pounds.' he replied whilst rephrasing the original question about justification for staff overtime.

Reading from the small print in an exercise book, he announced;

'Marketing is a mess. The records are incomplete, un-coordinated and unsatisfactory in detail and content.'

'All of this' he said 'would be forgivable if it was backed up by results. But it isn't. The sum total of business gained by purely local initiative is negligible. It is well below the level expected of unit managers.'

He turned over a page after licking his thumb. 'Quite often' he said 'we come up against the situation where a unit manager is not strong on the documentation side of his marketing campaign. But he compensates for this weakness by pulling in an above average share of the local functions business.

'That situation,' he announced 'is acceptable.'

'Here' he stated 'it does not apply. The records of calls made, follow-ups made, future bookings to chase and sales literature mailed is, at best, confused, at worst, negligent.'

'And the level of local functions held on the premises?'

'Well below par.' He answered his own question.

'Immediate improvement in detail, content and application' said Liaison imperiously, 'is a must do.'

'More initiative and direction' he said 'is a can do.'

'Direct management involvement' he continued 'is a will do.'

'Looking at the House,' he continued after turning another page, 'we find a similar vein of insufficient attention to detail applies.'

'You have fallen into the trap,' said Liaison' of assuming that room occupancy is the criteria by

215

which you are judged. There is,' he conceded grudgingly 'some truth in this if your hotel is one of those rare creatures which is in demand for seven days every week.'

He paused, pensively.

'But this is no such creature. It is busy for four days every week. A time when demand exceeds supply. A time when sales must be maximised to compensate for the next three days when the hotel will be less than half full. So, if you cannot generate you own week-end business, you can compensate a little by maximising your Monday to Thursday trade.'

'This is something you are failing to do.' he said.

He turned another page. It made a sharp, crackling noise.

'We cite' he said 'the week before last.'

'You had a three day sales conference here. Thirty-five delegates and day visitors. They did not share rooms when they could have been encouraged to do so. On the Wednesday night you were 12 overbooked. On Thursday night you were 17 overbooked. You referred them all to another hotel. They could all have slept here.'

'We know this to be so. We have contacted the course organiser and he would have agreed to room sharing for his delegates. You could have offered a reduced price as an incentive. He would have accepted your offer, had you made it.'

'If you had noticed this small detail,' he said 'your room occupancy would be the same. But your sales would have increased by several hundreds of pounds.'

'There was an opportunity presented' he said 'to offer a discounted rate to the friends and wives of all delegates for the week-end. You failed to seize this initiative. I have spoken to the organiser and I know that many would have accepted such an offer.'

'Yet another example of a wasted opportunity.' he said acidly
.
'But surely,' I protested, 'you have to give credit where it is due?'

'And just where would that be?'

'What about the Transition Tours account? It was me that introduced them to Happy Havens.'

'On the contrary,' said liaison spitefully,' Transition Tours have been a client company for many years. The only unusual aspect of the party that stayed here is the distance they travelled from Heathrow. Normally, Transition Tours use our airport hotels for delayed flights. So you succeeded in diverting business from one of the group's hotels to another.'

'Sonofabitch.' I said very slowly. I couldn't think of anything else to say that expressed my feeling of chagrin.

Liaison glared at me. 'Had you succeeded in diverting business here from a competitor, we would have commended your initiative. As it stands, you gain and the manager of the Airport Happy Haven loses.'

'Now give your attention to another aspect of the house which shows us up in a bad light.'

'I refer' he said 'to the strong possibility that rooms in the hotel are used improperly during several nights of the week.'

I opened my mouth to protest;

'Don't interrupt me again!!' liaison snapped.

'During our stay here our suspicions were aroused by a continuous shortage of sheets, towels and pillow-cases reported by the Housekeeper.'

I just had to contest that old chestnut from Iceberg.

'Listen........ .' I said.

'Just shut up, Hammond,' barked Liaison, 'just shut up and listen.' It was the first time that he had raised his voice above normal conversation tone. I was shocked into silence by the change of tone. The other members of the Wrecking Crew looked on impassively.

'So we took stock ourselves,' he continued 'and found that all shortages occurred during the nights when the regular Night Manager was on duty. There were no shortages of linen when the relief

Manager was on, so we concentrated on the nights when Travers was duty Night Manager.'

I could feel a numbness creeping over my body. Travers, stalwart Night Manager, dependable, problem solving Travers, the one who let me sleep soundly whilst he sorted out drunks, key-swipe losers, early risers, late arrivals and pre-dawn breakfasts. Travers, who even looked like a paragon of virtue! Avuncular, jovial, helpful and kindly Travers who kept watch over several hundred sleeping souls every night like a guardian nanny, was, in a word, bent.

'We are making the charitable assumption,' liaison continued 'that the rooms he let for short term use were to sleepers who paid him in cash. There are no records of room lets or receipts for cash from Travers during the period of surveillance. All the rooms had clean linen by the following morning.'

'Of course', liaison said, 'you must confront him with the evidence and accept his resignation immediately.'

I shook my head very slowly. I exhaled a long sigh.

'He was the most trustworthy of all the staff here. I wonder what caused him to become dishonest? And when it all started?'

'How long has the Housekeeper been reporting linen shortages?' asked liaison.

'Even since I have been here. Just over a year.'

'You should have put two and two together a long time ago.'

'I have lost my Bars Manager and now my Night Manager. Who can I trust? Are they all bent?'

'People are as dishonest as you let them be,' said Liaison, 'if you supervise them closely enough they don't get the chance to steal. Even if they do steal you catch them soon after. Then prosecute them. It discourages the others.'

Liaison was about to continue with his verbal report when a thought occurred to me.

'Why did you say earlier; we are making the charitable assumption that the rooms were let to sleepers?'

Liaison put down his note-book with a heavy sigh.

'I would have thought, Hammond, that the only other conclusion would be obvious, even to you!'

'Why should it be obvious?'

'Because, Hammond, there is only one other category of people who need hotel rooms for a short time during the night. With frequent changes of linen?' He made an upward movement with the palm of his hand, encouraging thought.

'You mean....................' Another shaft of blinding light was flooding into my dappled world..
Without waiting for me to finish the sentence, Liaison grated;

'That's right, Hammond, prostitutes. Male and female, black and white, all sizes and shapes. All bad for business in a hotel. The only one who gained from it all was your man Travers. He was running a private bordello right underneath your nose!'

I cast my mind back to many late night patrols through the hotel floors. Punters were always on the move, seeking rooms. lifts, services or information. Some were happy, some were morose. Some sought solace, some sought mischief. To me they were just punters, ordinary punters. I do not have the perception or experience to seek out the dishonest intuitively. One corridor full of punters is much the same as another corridor full of punters. If some of them were selling bodies I would not be able to tell the difference.

The message that I was getting from the Wrecking Crew was the same message that I had got from Jaysee; 'Don't trust anyone!'

Sadly, it seemed that the cynics were right about trust. I had given it to my colleagues. They had betrayed it. Now I stood accused of trusting colleagues. I had to answer for the losses that followed from abused trust.

I had an even bigger problem, too. If I could not trust any of my colleagues, how could I do my job? I needed their co-operation and support to run a 24/7 business which went on all day every day without stopping. When could I relax if I had to check on every transaction that took place? Who could I rely on? Pinky and Perky? Chef? Iceberg? Ethel?

'Can I go on now?' Liaison was getting testy again I nodded assent.

'Turning now to the Food and Bev department,' he read from his notes,' we find the same comments to be applicable.'

'Insufficient attention to detail and failure to adhere to the procedure laid down in the Manual has caused problems. The Food Operation is unusual. It uses more food than it should but does not offer superb value for money.'

I opened my mouth to say something. I had second thoughts and kept silent. Unperturbed Liaison continued;

'As an example of bad portion control and it's consequences, you should be aware that the English Breakfast served here does not yield the correct profit margin. This happens because you always serve two fried eggs with every Breakfast. The Catering Manifesto makes it abundantly clear that two eggs are served with three rashers of bacon only when Bacon and Eggs are ordered .... he recited a litany of permutations between bacon, eggs, mushrooms. fried bread, tomatoes and black pudding that sounded like a bingo caller's spiel. I didn't really hang on his every word as I was wondering whether one or two fried eggs really justified that amount of executive attention.

'This oversight alone' said Liaison, 'is forgivable if all other aspects of the Food Operation are perfect.'

That sounded quite optimistic. My optimism was quickly squashed when he said;

'Sadly, they are not.'

'The sum total of overcosting at Breakfast alone exceeds £12,000 a year.' His nostrils quivered as though he had detected a bad smell.

'Similar laxity in portion control did apply to all the meals served. The sum total of overcosting every year would exceed £26,000 a year if it continued.'

He glared at me over the top of his notebook.

'Much of this overcosting will cease now that my colleague here'..... he waved regally to Food and Bev; 'has instructed your chef in the correct interpretation of the Catering Manifesto.'

So far so good, I said to myself, just a small problem put right.

'To compound the failure,' said Liaison 'we find that the amount of money deducted from accommodation rates for breakfast is too low. It should be £8 per sleeper. Your local charge is £6.50 which is last year's rate.'

'We did find' Liaison continued' that most other meal rates were correctly charged.'

I managed to suppress a smug smile. It was small praise, but most welcome.

I was still basking in this glow when his next announcement came at me like grapeshot.

'The exception to this rule is the special functions. The rate here is understated on the books. The treatment of the service charge is suspect. It is credited to food instead of wages. It is throwing a false food percentage which, coupled with an understated stock level, indicates a manipulated result.'

'Oh shit' I said.

Liaison glared at me balefully. His rebuke was not as severe as the one that I handed myself. 'Martin Hammond' I said to myself, 'you have blown it.' These bastards have caught you bang to rights. They will nail you to the wall, balls and all, and leave the pieces out for crow bait. I waited for the handcuffs to appear. For the formal charge to be read out. I tried to remember the name of a solicitor who would spring me from the slammer.

'Do I still have your attention?' asked liaison irritably.

'Yes' I said faintly 'you have my undivided attention.'

He turned another page.

'On the other hand' he said 'we find the liquor operation to be well conducted, with ample stock levels and a reasonable turn round of wines, all yielding correct margins.'

I was still trying to register that one when he said; 'However, we are unable to agree the stock results over the last six months as the retail price of several items were understated.'

'When this error is rectified, we find that the results over the last six months show a small surplus instead of the deficit declared.'

'Would you?' I said slowly, 'run that one past me again? Slowly.'

He repeated it, word for word, without demur.

If I had not been sitting down I think I would have fallen down. He was telling me, in his dry unequivocal prose, that the Bars Manager was innocent after all. And I had hounded him, with Jaysee's backing, until he left!

This was turning out to be one of the worst days so far. It was easier to deal with overbooked punters. At least they had the honesty to shout and swear at me, to release their pent up anger in a stream of personal abuse. Suddenly I found myself in a world full of deception, intrigue and subterfuge. Nobody wore their true colours. The apparently honest were crooked. The crooks were honest men in disguise. And I was blindfold in their midst, harassing the straight and encouraging the bent. All was revealed in the pitiless glare of the Wrecking Crew's searchlight.'

'The last part of our study' said Liaison,' was concerned with Control.'

They must have had difficulty finding fault there, I thought. Ibrahim, my assiduous, portly Pakistani control clerk spent all day filling in forms, completing summaries, finalising returns, addlisting totals. He was always busy in his tiny office. He stayed late into the night to finish his work, long beyond his departure time.

Maybe I would hear some good news from the Wrecking Crew this time? I settled down to listen.

'We found the Control Department to be weak, lax and bordering on the dishonest.'

'You must be joking' I said.

Liaison sighed and looked at his watch.

'We never joke' he said, ' and no more interruptions, please.'

He emphasised 'Please'. I figured that he had a train to catch. Much of his display of pique might be attributable to impatience rather than irritation. Maybe he wasn't a hit-man after all. His team had uncovered some pretty nasty truths about my Happy Haven. But he seemed reluctant to do anything about it. There was enough evidence in his portfolio to justify a Kangaroo Court with me as the first victim, closely followed by the Night Manager. Very shortly I would hear why the Control Clerk was on the short list for hanging too.

But Liaison seemed intent on just talking about it, like an auditor. His armament was all verbal, it lacked teeth. I relaxed a little. I can take any amount of verbal mauling. I have had many hours of practice at just listening to words which are intended to hurt. By comparison with a really wound-up overbooking, Liaison was an amateur.

Liaison turned over another page.
'Petty Cash expenditure is high for a unit of this size. The expenditure on postage is also out of step with the Marketing campaign. There are no postal records worth a damn.'

'Casual wages paid out are too high, with indistinct names and addresses which could not be traced. On many of the authorisations for payment of Casual wages there is a facsimile of your signature which is probably forged.'

'There are many payments for late night taxis to take staff home. The records do not show who went where, and why the journey was necessary.'.

'Banking of cash and cheques takes longer than is necessary. Just a couple of days, you understand, but enough to arouse our suspicions when coupled with the Casual wage and late night taxi query.'

'But worst of all,' said Liaison sonorously 'your debtors are not called in fast enough. There are accounts going back four, five and six months which should have been sent to Head Office for action long ago. Some are probably bad debts by now, but we have yet to establish whether they are genuine debts or not. Accounts will be looking into this very soon.'

'Local payments for food are also suspect. The amounts are not supported by invoice to Happy Havens. Some receipts are from local supermarkets and probably refer to personal shopping. All the suspect receipts are authorised by your signature which is probably forged.'

'Outside the Control Office' said liaison 'we found the forward reservation system to be adequate rather than expert, the allocation of rooms to be arbitrary, the Standard Room Inventory to be incomplete, stock levels of food to be understated and the supervision of stores non-existent.'

He closed his notebook and looked at his watch again.

'Do you?' I said 'by any chance have any good news for me'

'Yes I do,' he said, 'and some more bad news too.'

'Let me have it that order, will you?'

His expression changed very slightly. I think it was a smile.

'The good news is........... we are leaving.'

His team all gave their interpretation of a smile. It varied from a grimace to a wince.

'And the bad news?' I asked.

'Your former Bars Manager is suing you and the company for Unfair Dismissal.'

' .... and as a summary of all that has been said' Liaison droned on ' please read you Manual and Operating Procedures.'

'Every single item' he said 'that I have drawn to your attention is contained in the Manual -your Bible.'

'Make it compulsory bed-time reading' he said' and you will probably never see me again.'

The Wrecking Crew shook hands with me, one by one.
Then they filed out of my office, leaving the door open.

CHAPTER 16 RETRIBUTION

In the Far East, when they want to let you know that your days are numbered, they send you bantam feathers. The Latin countries send you a knotted purple ribbon. The more sophisticated branches of the Mafia send you an engraved invitation to your own funeral.

In Happy Havens, they send you a Green Copy Memorandum. The original goes to Walter himself.

On balance, I would rather have the feathers, ribbon or invitation. At least it shows that they are coming to get you. The Green Copy is an invitation to dig your own grave and jump into it.

The first warning shot was fired by Casino Chips. He swallowed a summary of amendments prepared by the Wrecking Crew, suffered a bout of electronic dyspepsia and spewed out a Quallfied Trading Summary.

This lengthy and wordy document was ablaze with upper case caps in violent shades of red, purple and vermilion. Ordinary corrections were just underlined. More blatant amendments were swathed in red. Serious re-adjustments were highlighted in purple. Unpardonable sins were encased in vermillion coffins. This lengthy tirade of electronic indignation was e/mailed around Head Office, emphasising it's urgency by the heading ; Private & Confidential Green Copy, Limited Circulation Only.

Head Office pundits, known by initials only, stroked their goatee beards, spoke to each other by intercom and conferred in the Executive loo. Casino Chips had that effect on ordinary mortals.

'Don't like the sound of this at all,' was the general opinion,

'Better get a Green Copy off to this man Hammond and ask him to explain.'

When the shit is about to hit the fan, it is very important indeed to be standing in the most sheltered position. So the Green Copies began to appear in my daily mail delivery.

Jaysee wanted to know about my amended Food Results and 'sought enlightenment' about the Night Manager's activities.'

Legal and Secretarial wanted chapter and verse about the visit by the Trading Standards Officer.

Personnel sought 'clarification' on the circumstances leading to the Bars Manager's resignation.

Accounts were to carry out an 'interim audit' to disclose the extent of fraud in the Control Office.

Even Emdeo joined the lynch mob. His Green Copy announced that he was 'puzzled and upset' by my post-course assessment.

****

'You got' said Naomi over dinner, 'two choices, baby.'

'Which are?'

'Either you put it so right that none can ever criticise you again.'

'Or?'

'You quit.'

'Nothing in between those two?' I asked hopefully.

'No.'

'What do you think, Louis?'

We were dining at Louis' Restuarant, away from the intrigue of my Happy Haven. Nearly all the customers at Louis had gone home, leaving us alone amongst the empty tables.

'I think the time has come for you and Happy Havens to part company, Marty,' You can resign and write it off to experience. If you resign, there's an end of it. If you stay, you may be dismissed. It will be much harder to explain to another group why you were dismissed. Far easier to say that you had a dis-agreement with your boss and left.'

'If I do resign,' I said fiercely, 'I will know exactly what not to do next time.'

'How's that?' asked Naomi.

'I will never, ever trust anybody again. Not when my job depends on it.'

'You gotta have trust, Mardi. Without it, your life will be impossible.'

'Well,' I said, 'it is going to be difficult to trust anyone again. Too many people have let me down.'

'Aw, come on, Mardi', said Naomi, 'that just ain't true. You were set up by two people only. The Night Manager and the Control Clerk. The rest were always straight and loyal.'

Very tactfully, she did not mention the Bars Manager.

'Well' I said, mollified, 'if you put it like that, I have to admit that the rest were always on my side. They didn't let me down. But I can't help feeling that somehow I have let them down.'

'Everyone makes mistakes,' said Naomi, 'nobody is right all the time.'

'But some make bigger mistakes than others.' I added.

She patted my hand fondly; 'It goes with the territory, baby. The bigger the job, the bigger the booboo.'

'Problems,' I said, 'I got. Solutions, I ain't.'

233

'Sleep on it, Marty,' said Louis, , do nothing for the time being. ' 'Something unexpected will turn up and you will forget all about it.'

It seemed like good advice. We went home and slept on it. Naomi left early the following morning to go to Brittany, France and Flanders, Belgium.

'Whatever you decide to do, sweetheart', she said 'I am with you all the way.'

'I have a score to settle with Happy Havens,' I said 'for both of us.'

'Take it easy, baby,' she said, relax a little.'

'I know,' I said 'just let your balls hang out.'

CHAPTER 17 REVENGE

The Head Office of Happy Haven Hotels is located in Central London. Another one of those impassive fingers pointing at the sky, gaining in height what it lacks in style, rooted in scurry and exhaust fumes with it's blind head feeling the clouds.

Easy to see, but not easy on the eye, expedient but unattractive, efficient in a functional way, a monument to convenience, command and control. And much larger and more formidable than I remembered it to be.

I had visited Happy Havens Head Office once before. To be interviewed for my first management job. The impression I gained then was of a tall building with high speed lifts, a honeycomb of identical offices, soothing background music and a proliferation of fresh flowers in unlikely places.

This time I saw a huge building with uniform tinted eyes staring blankly at the neighbouring towers, deflecting the world outside and screening the private world inside. A private world full of Happy Haven executives who wanted to see me in the flesh. To seek explanations, to be enlightened, to resolve mysteries or to account for some anomaly or other that puzzled them. The terminology changed according to the department, but the message spelt out on Green Copy Memos was the same; explain what happened and exonerate me from all blame. Help the executive to c.y.a (cover it's ass).

I had given myself up to this examination by my Lords and Masters voluntarily. The defence that I could offer for my corporate misdeeds was slight. I could offer ignorance, youth and bad luck as my excuse, but not a lot else. On balance, the chances of success against the united ranks of my accusers were slight. The corporate ranks of Happy Havens had closed against me, screened by a paper wall of Green Copy Memos. By comparison, Don Quixote had been in with a better chance against the windmills.

'The components of a successful plan,' came a whisper from a past course, 'are who does what, where, when and how. The why should be known in advance.' I had worked out the what and the who all right. It was the where, when and why that had eluded me.

'Never become confused about the ends and the means' the same lecturer had said. 'They are not the same, and must be approached in different ways.' Another bombshell of logic which had eluded me down at the sharp end.
I would lay my future plans more carefully, bolstered by first hand experience of what not to do.

So I approached my Head Office with a steely resolve, determined to acquit myself well, even if it was a losing battle that I was fighting.

Unbeknown to my judges, I had a private score to settle with one of them. Someone with a goatee beard, whose telephone number was known by heart to Naomi-Naomi Dwight from Nantucket, Nantucket Island. Someone who had hurt and humiliated her a long time ago. Someone who had insulted and rejected her callously, leaving a scar which had taken a long time to heal. Someone whose name had not been revealed to me in spite of my insistent questions.

Someone we did not talk about any more, but who was the focus of my present rage.

'You judge a man by the manner of his departure,' echoed through my mind as I approached the entrance to Head Office.

Happy Bloody Haven Hotels would remember this day, and Martin Hammond too, I resolved.

The receptionist in the foyer was young and attractive, groomed to look like a debutante. She was surrounded by fresh flowers and smiled mechanically as I approached.

'Martin Hammond to see Legal and Secretarial.' I said, by-passing the formalities, 'I have an appointment.'

'On the twenty second floor' she said.

'Have a nice day, Mr Hammond' she added as I walked away.'

I looked at her suspiciously to see if she was mocking me.

She wasn't.

'The lift is in the middle of the foyer' she said, pointing.

CHAPTER 18 REGRET

Something about the corridors of Head Office was vaguely familiar. They bore a family likeness to the corridors of Happy Haven Hotels. Not identical, like twins, more like the perceived similarity between mother and daughter.

The carpets were the same. A house blend of H.H.H. blended from dark brown into even darker brown. The blurb racks were the same, overflowing with multi coloured brochures pushing Happy Havens as a universal panacea for travellers itch. The smoke doors and vending machines were the same. The people looked the same, moving purposefully along, avoiding eye or body contact with sub-conscious skill.

Then it dawned on me. Head Office was different because all the doors were open. Hotels sell privacy to people who hide away from the hordes. Head Office was open-ended and buzzing like a bee-hive.

Legal and Secretarial have their allotted space in the hive. It was portioned by potted plants which grew thick and green to the ceiling, dappled by diffused light from slatted blinds. It looked like a jungle clearing where earnest young Administrators were wrestling with the native problem.

The ardent young man who interviewed me was surrounded by a battery of heavy legal text books.

He sighed heavily, overcome by intensity.

'This, then, is a fair summary of what happened, Mr Hammond.'

'H.M. Inspectorate' -we had already established that what he referred to as H M Inspectorate was, in my language, the TSO, 'called unannounced at the Cocktail Bar of the Happy Haven at approximately 19.30 on Sunday, 23rd October and asked for a whisky?'

I nodded assent.

'The whisky was dispensed by your former Bars Manager, Mr Albert Gordon Platt, who, at the time, was employed under contract by this company.'

He dotted the i's and crossed the t's in his mind.

'H M Inspectorate accepted the whisky. He tendered the exact payment for the whisky as indicated by the tariff board on display. The same tariff display also indicated the measure served.' He sucked his teeth noisily.

'H M Inspectorate then declared his interest and informed the dispenser of his name, identity and departmental address.'

'He told him who he was,' I said helpfully.

The legal and secretarial brow knitted into even closer concern.

'H M Inspectorate then produced his brief case and proceeded to test the liquid dispensed for quantity and provenance.'

'That's right,' I said cheerfully, 'he stuck his gadget innit.'

Legal and Secretarial, known as Elbee to his colleagues, agonised. He grimaced and clasped his hairless chin. He looked like a child who refuses to open up for the dentist. 'He then informed the company's secretariat,' he muttered 'of his findings and confirmed this opinion by secondary and tertiary analysis.' A pall of depression hung over his desk.

'Subsequently,' he said brightly, 'he confirmed his findings in writing to the joint holders of the liquor license.'

'You've got it, baby,' I said 'in a nutshell.'

I gave him a broad and knowing wink. He looked at me in astonishment.

'I do not understand what you mean' he said 'this is a serious matter and you are treating it much too flippantly.'

'They have got us,' I said 'bang to rights. We are over the proverbial barrel and we will be busted by the law.'

'So it would appear' he said drily, 'I will enter an appearance on behalf of the joint licensees and put forward a plea in mitigation. I cannot, of course, hold out any real hope of an acquittal.'

He looked at me nervously. The way you would look at truculent drunks. I leaned over his desk very slowly,and I fixes him in an unblinking stare. He stared at me with widened eyes.

'Now hear this' I said when our noses nearly met, 'you gotta get me and my buddy off this rap, see? We don't wanna go inside, we ain't gonna do time. See this guy, and make him an offer he can't refuse.'

I walked out of the legal and secretarial jungle before he could think of any more statements to translate into legal gobbledegook.

I began to enjoy my second and probably last day in Happy Havens Head Office.

The need for deference had faded away. These people were my former masters. They did not control my life anymore so it was a time for frank talking, no longer hindered by the need to pussyfoot and toady to commandants.

I was armoured by a letter in my breast pocket which made me bulletproof.

Neatly typed and succinct, the letter required my signature and the date to become my farewell to Happy Havens. It was a standard letter of resignation, my release from contract, my escape from responsibility, my get out from the web of red tape wound so tightly around me by the money spiders of Head Office.

I would present it at the exact moment needed to give it full impact. To the person who deserved it most, further down my visiting list.

CHAPTER 19 REMORSE

I went through the door marked 'Personnel' into another simulated rain forest.

This office had more credibility than Legal and Secretarial. The receptionist was a charming shade of *cafe au lait*. A brilliant sari hung in loose folds from her shoulders, but did not disguise the sensual curves beneath as she rose to greet me.

'Good morning' she said, all musk and meekness. Disarmed by her serenity, I lowered my aggression threshold.

'Martin Hammond, to see Seajay.'

'The Personnel Director is expecting you,' she said softly, 'but he has someone with him at the moment.' 'Would you like something to drink whilst you are waiting?'

I thought about my strategy for winding up Seajay. Then I decided that I didn't have one. It would come about naturally, I decided.

Seajay peered at me over a pile of paper in the middle of his desk. He was a short fat man. His lack of height was exaggerated by a tall desk or a short chair. His head was lower than the top of his chair, and his ears stuck out like air scoops. He looked puzzled.

'Did you see that lady who just left here?'

'No' I replied, lying in my teeth just to get things started.

'Most extraordinary, most extraordinary. Never seen anything like it in my life.'

'She looked all right to me,' I said, hoping he would pick up on the fib.

'She came in for an interview,' he said, staring at a picture on the far wall, 'for a job as Housekeeper.'

'Funny breed, those,' I sympathised, thinking of Iceberg.

I don't think he heard me.

'She has all the right qualifications for the job. Good background, good training, first class experience, excellent track record.'
'There wasn't a single doubt in my mind. She was Happy Haven material, without a doubt.'

'So what's the problem?'

He shifted uncomfortably in his chair and nearly disappeared behind the pile of paper.

'What would you do if you were in my position?'

I suppressed the temptation to suggest sitting on a cushion.

'Probably the same as you?' I hedged. 'Most difficult, most dificult.' he muttered. A long silence followed whilst he pondered the problem. The

244

White Rabbit in Alice in Wonderland was a better decision maker than Seajay.

'You still haven't told me what the problem is'

He looked at me curiously, as if I was an unexploded bomb with a spluttering fuse.

'When the interview was over, I offered her the job subject to the usual conditions of references and status.'

'So what's the problem?' I asked again.

'She accepted the job. Then she said did I mind if she smoked.'

'And that's your problem?'

I thought again of Iceberg, rigid and unforgiving in her starched Calvinistic ways. Maybe she had a secret vice too, carefully concealed inside a sanitised closet somewhere. I wondered which one it could possibly be.

Seajay agonised again. 'She lit a cigar,' he said, 'a huge dark brown Havana'.
'
I tried to think of Iceberg smoking a cigar. Somehow, it did not gel..

'You should be grateful for small mercies,' I said, 'it might have been an Afghani Black and she could have gone for a trip round the moon.'

Seajay looked alarmed. 'I think,' he said 'that I had better send off a covering letter. On the other hand, though, that might be considered to be discriminatory.'

He shook his head unhappily and hopped back into Wonderland again. Apart from a convulsive fidget and a marked facial tic he remained incommunicado for several minutes.

Eventually I said; 'Is'nt it uncomfortable for you?'

'What? What did you say?' He came back to the present with a jerk.

'I said; is'nt it uncomfortable?'

'What? what do you mean, uncomfortable?'

'Sitting like you are,' I said 'must be uncomfortable.'

He looked at me as if I had just made a rude noise. His nostrils twitched.

'Why should it be uncomfortable?'

'When you have a leg on both sides of the fence, it most be quite uncomfortable. There is always a danger that a fence post might get stuck up your butt.'

Seajay looked around nervously, seeking moral support from inanimate objects.

'What is it,' he said 'that I can do for you, Mr Hammond?'

'It's the other way around.' I replied, 'more a question of what I can do for you.'

'You can do something for me?'

We seemed to be getting nowhere fast, so I spelt it out for him.'

'Bars Manager -T.S.O. -watered whisky -ding-dong -heave-ho -pain in the ass. Unfair dismissal- Industrial Tribunal-Green Copy -I'm all yours baby.'

'Ah yes,' he said, visibly relieved, 'Albert Gordon Platt.' Former Bars Manager at your Happy Haven.' Taking us to an Industrial Tribunal claiming Constructive Dismissal.' he said unhappily, 'got it all in the file here.'

'I thought it was Unfair Dismissal he was claiming?' What's the difference.'

He brightened up a little, on firmer ground now.

'Unfair Dismissal arises' he announced 'when you dismiss an employee for what you consider to be valid reasons. If he or she does not agree with your reasons an Industrial Tribunal will rule on it.'

'That doesn't apply in this case. He resigned.'

'Quite so' said Seajay primly, 'that is why he is claiming Constructive Dismissal.'

'So there is a difference?'

'When an employee claims Constructive Dismissal,' said Seajay, 'it is because he or she believes that the job was made untenable by undue pressure.'

'What used to be called leaning on people?'

'That's right, just about right' said Seajay in his lecturing mode, 'nowadays it's a no-no.'

I took that lot on board and wondered if it applied to me. It was just possible to argue that I had been leaned on and pressurized by Jaysee, the Wrecking Crew and Head Office.

'So what do we do about Alfred Gordon Platt?' I asked.

'It is early days, yet' said Seajay.' I want to hear the full story from you before deciding which way to go.'

I told the sad and unhappy tale of Albert Gordon Platt. I made no attempt to whitewash my own part in the story but I did cast Jaysee as the villain of the piece.

Seajay made copious notes throughout.

'He has a very good case, you know.' he said ' your reasons for wanting him to leave were unsound. The report from Special Projects proves that.'

He looked at his notes intently.

'This incident with the bottle of watered whisky .... you can't prove his connection with it. All he did was sell it. He can't be held responsible for what was in the bottle, that's for sure. '

'In which case' he mused out loud 'the Tribunal will almost certainly find for him.'

'What,' I asked 'are you going to do about it, then?'

I felt detached from it all, as though it was happening to someone else. Away from the scene of the dispute, on the 23rd floor of a tall office in London, it all seemed academic. I could see, with Olympian breadth of vision, that someone had made a monumental cock-up down below. It would surely end in tears, but just who would shed the tears was unclear. I could spare some for Albert Gordon Platt, former Bars Manager unjustly accused of dishonesty. But Jaysee should weep a bucketful, he had started the *vendetta*.

'If he sees it through to the end,' said Seajay, 'he will be given compensation for loss of earnings and damages.'

'What happens,' I asked 'if he gets another job before the hearing?'

'The Tribunal will take that into account. He will be awarded the difference between his old and new entitlement. Plus damages, of course.'

'I see,' I said, wondering if my own job came into the same category, 'I see.'

'Of course,' said Seajay expansively, 'we always have the option to settle out of court. We could design a package between ourselves.'

'How much would that be?' I tried to sound casual and disinterested.

'Can't possibly say.' Seajay shrugged. 'it varies from case to case. It is a lottery, really. Varies from a few hundred to several thousands.'

I tried to be unmoved. I failed.

'You could do a deal with him. I always found him to be reasonable.'

'That really does not sound like grounds for dismissing him, does it?'

'Water under the bridge by now,' I said, 'I know that I have blown it. I confess that I made a balls of it. But I know that it will all come right.'

'How do you know that?' Seajay was becoming edgy again.

'Because you are such a clever chap, Seajay.' I said' a smart arse without equal. If anyone can do it, you can. I bet you can grind the poor bastard down to a shadow of his former self and make him settle for half of what he is entitled to.'

I wondered if this was the right moment to lay my resignation on his desk. I decided that it was not.

'It's all very well for you chaps,' Seajay said, 'you can just go around driving a coach and horses through Employment legislation. I'm the one who has to pick up the pieces afterwards. Nobody ever gives me any sympathy or help. I just have to get on with it all by myself.'

'if you think this is tough, Seajay, you should try it down at the sharp end.'

'Nobody appreciates what I do for them. I am taken for granted by all.' He looked dejected and very vulnerable in his oversize chair.

'Seajay.' I said dramatically, 'that just ain't true!'

I stood up very suddenly, ready to make a half rehearsed speech.

'For I have heard it said, in the remotest corners of the Happy Haven empire, that there is a man in Head Office who stands up to be counted for his untiring defence of the rights of the common man, and common woman, the ordinary employee, the spearchuckers who eek out a precarious existence in the bowels of huge hotels.'

He looked around desperately, seeking an escape.

'To these poor souls, these huddled masses,' I projected minority group concern, 'often alone, despised and exploited by a system of monumental inhumanity, one name, and one name alone, is on their lips, held in their hearts as a hope for a brighter future, cherished as an ideal which may be achieved in their children's lifetime.'

Seajay looked ready to bolt. I stood between him and the door which was guarded by a gentle Asian lady.

I pointed an accusing finger at his head. 'When commis cooks and assistant room maids meet in clandestine copulation on the mountains of soiled linen in the Laundry Room late at night, what do you think they talk about?'

'I haven't the faintest idea.' gasped Seajay.

'They talk,' I said between clenched teeth, 'of Seajay, Director of Personnel at Head Office, continuing his lonely crusade against the inequality of a system which grinds men into robots and keeps them remote from the better things in life like Acid House parties, The X Factor, Eastenders, Tom and Jerry and Match of the Day.

'Denied these privileges,' I said, 'they are incomplete, unaware and doomed to become social outcasts, the rejects of society, shamed by their inability to become football hooligans, lager louts or Members of Parliament.'

I led him back gently to his oversize chair.

'Don't let them down, Seajay, they depend on you.

I slapped his wobbly cheeks twice, very softly. Then I kissed the top of his head, a loud and wet smacker.

'Keep up the good works,' I said.

With my fist clenched and aloft I left his office.

En route for Accounts.

CHAPTER 20 REVIEW

Accounts dwelt at another level, in another slice of time. Not for them the heavy jungle growth, the monsoon oppression of the para-tropics. They favoured the serried rank and file of work stations, linked by conveyor belts to mark out their borders..

Heads down in fixed concentration, the number crunching operators focused on their VDU's, sifting the grist for Casino Chips's data diet.

The majority of the operators were Asian and female. Their fingers ran fleetly over pale keyboards, sending out staccato messages which were acknowledged by faint electronic monotones.

Curiosity outranked culture momentarily as I walked in. The cicada pulse faded as gold stars on dark brown brows glistened in the harsh light, staring at a stranger.

Then it was eyes down, and back to bingo.

The Head of Accounts office was at the far side of this Oriental magic bazaar. I went round the edges lest my wake should cause ripples in that exotic weave

'I have recast your summaries to date,' said Accounts, 'in the light of the updated information sent to me by Special Projects.'

'When I followed this amended Audit Trail,' he continued, looking at me like an effigy on a tomb, ' it turned out that your budget cumulative to date is incorrect only in terms of detail and margin. The volume is unchanged as we were led to believe that these errors arose as a result of incorrect postings in principle rather than quantity.'

He looked at me expectantly.

'Would you,' I said 'accept an unqualified remark from me?'

'Of course' said Accounts.

'I haven't the faintest idea what you are talking about.'

'I am talking,' he said patiently, 'about your figures.'

'If that is so, ' I said' you are not using any language that I understand.'

'I have a fluent command of six European languages,' I lied, 'and what you have just said is not in any of them. Kindly translate for the benefit of a simpleton.'

'Ah' he said, 'ah yes.'

'Now tell me again. And this time in a language that we both understand.'

Accounts was quite good as an interpreter. He told me that during my trading year to date my food percentage was in the upper fifties, 'with an occasional dip into the lower fifties and the odd excursion to the lower sixties.'

'Very much as I would expect,' he confided, 'with some peaks and some troughs.'

'The average spend per head on accommodation has been amended downwards, but not dramatically. It is still O.K.'

'About par for the course.' he said.

The liquor results had also been vindicated by the same internal magic. All this had been achieved, Accounts assured me, by over-riding Casino Chips and working it all out manually.

'All in all' said Accounts, looking at me over half-moon glasses, 'a middle of the road, average performance. Nothing spectacular, nothing to be ashamed of either. The majority of our hotels turm in this sort of result.'

'Anything else you would like to know?'

It was ironic that I came to Head Office for the second time in my career as a defendant, with my resignation burning a hole in my breast pocket.

Defending myself against what? An average, lack lustre performance with room for improvement, no denying that. But the vilification and accusations of incompetence heaped upon my head by a bunch of Head Office Hitlers was really out of all proportion to the crime.

I had been faulted by a system as blind and deaf as it's founders. A system which registered shadows but ignored sunshine, a system which listened to the notes but did not hear the music. A purblind, half deaf oracle who published half truths which were taken as gospel.

'Casino Chips' I said out loud, 'you have a lot to answer for.'

Right now I was probably the only one who knew about it. I was probably the only one who cared about it, too. I did not have any more to say to Accounts. I left quietly, skirting around the borders of his harem.

CHAPTER 21 REBUKE.

John Price, El doubya doubya, Welsh demagogue and management evangelist was next on my list.

He lacked a department of any real substance to call his own. He was caged in a small room without benefit of foliage or secretarial minder.

Nothing at all to insulate him from casual callers. Maybe it was in his creed to be available at all times, like a Good Samaritan. Or maybe he was just lonely.

'I have always held to the belief -his chant was still compulsive, earnest and hypnotic -'that if you fail to understand me, it is because I failed to express myself correctly. Not because my listener is too stupid to understand, but because I failed to make my point clearly enough for him to understand my meaning fully.'

'You can't argue with that.' I said.

'So it came as a distinct shock to me,' he said' when I read your post-course report which suggested that the Food and Bev Control seminar was; long on entertainment and short on education.'

'What exactly,' he asked 'did you mean by that?'

'Is that what I wrote?'

'In black and white, buoyo, on your appraisal form.'

258

I tried to remember filling in his appraisal form. I failed. It was just another form, one of many that were churned out every week. About statistics, returns, drafts, minutes or budgets, sins of commission or omission, past boo-boos or misdemeanors, oversights or lapses. All Happy Haven forms have a small box at the bottom, marked; 'Manager's comments.'

Much earlier in my management career, I had been restrained and helpful with my comments. Then my misguided sense of the ridiculous took over. The little white boxes brought out the *graffiti* instinct. I began with with little asides, like 'Martin Hammond is innocent, O.K?' and 'Signed in His absence, by Cardinal Marker, secretary to......... .'

More recently, with a sense of impending doom, I had written *'Mea culpa'* and 'Extreme Unction requested.'

Everyone else in Head Office ignored my little foible. Except John Price, who had time to be offended.

'I was referring,' I said 'to the lack of social life on your courses.'

'When delegates are sent on courses,' he said snottily, 'it is not with the intention that they should be part of the social calendar. Their week is mapped out to give a good mix of lectures, projects and case studies. Any spare time comes about as a result of hard work and application. It should be used for healthy exercise and relaxation, not for indulging in wild parties and drinking to excess.

'The last time I heard that speech,' I said 'was from the Salvation Army in a pub full of dedicated boozers. 'don't knock the boozers, John,' I urged, 'they pay your wages and mine.'

'You are not making any sense, any sense at all.' he said.

'That is probably because,' I mimicked his Welsh accent, 'I failed to express myself correctly in the first place.'

He glared at me, glowing like a spent ember.

'In the event' I continued, 'all that I learned in five days was what not to do in certain circumstances and how to do something else that I should not do ever.'

'Do you understand me?'

'No.' he replied, the only time in his life when he used one word instead of twenty.

'Are you sitting comfortably? Then I'll explain.'

'You and all your cronies assume that you can teach us our business. And you probably can, providing it is theory you are talking about. Down at the sharp end, we have to learn new ways of doing things every day. The learning curve is very sharp indeed when you have to explain to a punter why he can't stay in your hotel. He gets mad and calls you very rude names. He gets personal and violent. He doesn't give a damn about the theory of overbooking. Sometimes you are called out in the middle of the night to sort out drunks and villains who are just looking for a fight. All the lessons in the world won't help you then. If you keep your cool you might just persuade him not to punch your face in, but no theory that I know of will help you out of that corner. You have to face your problems all by yourself, and invent the solution. There are no theories to pull you through.'

'I can see what you are getting at' he replied, settling down for a nice chat, 'but I still don't understand why you say that my courses are entertaining.'

'Your courses are entertaining, John, because I can only absorb a small amount of new information thoroughly. The rest just passes me by. I get bored. When I am bored, I invent little games to keep me awake.'

'I am not alone in this,' I said as he opened his mouth to debate the point.

'All the delegates felt the same way.'

'Don't interrupt me John,' I said as he tried to join in again, 'you are just about to learn something of great value to all theorists.'

'By day 5, we were all on overload. And we were probably a bit hung over, too. You were droning on about something which was quite important to you. It was going over our heads. So we played bingo instead.'

'You did what?' Emdeo was stunned into brevity.

'We played word bingo. It is really simple. You write down a word or phrase. Give it to your neighbour. He waits for a word which begins with the right letter. Then he crosses it off his card until it is complete.'

'That is juvenile and stupid ....'

'Whoa, John, whoa,' I said, 'I am just answering your question about entertainment.'

'Now you listen to me, Mr Manager,' Emdeo said, 'I am not going to sit here and let all this nonsense go on............... .'

'But I haven't told you the best bit yet,' I interrupted his flow, 'the one which won the first prize for the week.'
'The winner was,......' I paused for effect, 'Martin Hammond, who won first prize for the week with the well known phrase or saying .... John Price is a pompous prick.'

'And do you know,' I leaned forward in mock excitement, 'I got that in 17 minutes flat, John.'
'Do you think?' I asked 'that we should offer it to the Guinness Book of records. Or should it stay as an in-house competition?'

'This interview, Mr Manager,' John Price snapped, 'is finished. Kindly leave my office.' He stood by the door and held it wide open.

'You shouldn't take yourself so seriously, John,' I said on the way out, 'relax a little. Let your balls hang out.'

CHAPTER 22 REALITY.

The young lady who directed me to Jaysee's office said;

'Operations? Just go up a floor and the office is by the third vending machine on the left. It is quicker to walk.' She strode off purposefully, a maid with a mission.

The style of the Operations Office was different. Unlike the other cells in the hive, this one had a closed door. Entry was voluntary, no casual callers were welcome here.

Once inside, I saw shabby utilitarian well worn desks in drab olive .All the fittings . were robust and functional, welded into sympathy with a butch background.

Uncarpeted, unrelieved by pastel shades or any attempt to display frivolity, it looked like a barracks for the recruits of one of the less noble regiments.

Metal desks butted each other purposefully. Men whom I assumed to be District Managers bellowed and bawled into hand-sets, each trying to drown the other's hubbub. Like a classroom of boys with bellyache, they writhed and groaned, wriggled and winced until the act of ending the call released them from conflict. The air was made dense by testosterone and aggression, somehow oppressive and mildly hostile.

I remembered receiving telephone calls from Jaysee. Always with a background grumble like traffic near a flyover, muted and savage.

Jaysee saw me and waved. At least I thought it was a wave. He used the same action that drovers use when cracking a bull whip.
He pointed to a door away from the main office and headed for it. Deliberate and sure footed, like a trainer amongst his team.

Inside, with the door closed. the roar subsided like a spent wave.

'You owe me an explanation.' he said.

I was still in two minds about my resignation. As dilatory as a lover pulling petals off a flower, I could not yet say, 'I leave' or 'I leave not.'

I could end it here and now, or wait to be pushed right over the edge. Either way, I did not have to take any more stick from Jaysee.

'There are,' I said evenly, 'a couple of explanations that you owe me.'

'You mean about the Bars result?' he said, 'I have read the Special Projects report. It seems that we were both wrong about that.'

'That is not the way that I read it,' I said 'I would say that the blame for Platt's dismissal was 90% you and 10% me.'

'It is not the Dismissal that I am concerned about,' Jaysee said 'that will be resolved long before it comes to a Hearing. My real concern is with the most basic error of all. Using wrong retail prices. That is the part I find hardest to forgive.'

'Let me see ifI have got this right.' I said, 'it does'nt matter a tupenny damn if someone is sacked unfairly. But it is a federal offence to get your retail prices wrong?'

'If you had got your sums right in the first place, Hammond, then he would not have been dismissed at all, would he?'

'And if you had not told me that he was as bent as a corkscrew I would never have started the witch hunt in the first place.'

'It will not go to a Tribunal,' Jaysee repeated, 'it will be settled long before that.'

'So,' I said, as evenly as I could, 'it doesn't matter that he is sacked unfairly, it doesn't matter at all?'

'Not particularly,' Jaysee shrugged, 'the odds are well and truly stacked in his favour. He will come out ahead. Happy Havens will settle out of court and it won't even be charged to you. You can get another Bars Manager and learn from your mistake.'

'You mean,' I said bitterly, 'learn from your mistake.'

'As long as you learn, it doesn't matter whose experience you learn from.'

'So will you, Jaysee.' I said 'and you might also forget about your intuitive analysis of sales mix variations or any other technical crap which enables you to give such bum advice to unit managers.'

'Unit managers,' said Jaysee heavily, 'whose night managers run private bordellos need all the advice they can get.'

'Provided,' I said 'that the advice doesn't come from professional assholes.'

He flushed angrily.'Now look here.......... .' he began.

'No' I said' you look here. ' I have already spoken to four departments in this Kremlin of yours and you are the fifth. You all have this high-handed patronising attitude. You assume that all unit managers are mentally deficient buffoons without the wit or nous to run the hotels without your input of savvy and know-how.'

'Fair comment,' said Jaysee cooly, 'and about right.'

'So you tell all the managers that they are idiots. And you repeat it so often that they begin to believe it themselves.'

'Some managers,' said Jaysee spitefully, 'are more idiot than others.'

'And some district managers,' I said' are the misbegotten sons of cheap whores'

By now we were both standing eyeball to eyeball, poised to receive or throw the first punch. If either of us had moved a fraction of an inch after the first abrupt stand it would have become a serious fist fight.

Jaysee was scarlet from the neck up. I could see a vein throbbing in his temple. I knew that I had paled to a deathly white. Deathly white with glowing eyes.

Slowly, very slowly, Jaysee sank back into his chair. His colour returned to normal. Suddenly, he looked much older. His face was deeply scored, his eyes dull. He sagged from the shoulders. His large hands gripped the arms of his chair for support.

From my standing position anger gave way to a kind of pity. I knew that the confrontation was over. I began to shake violently. I could feel my heart pounding noisily and fast. I sat down, too. A long silence followed. For the first time that day I began to wonder if I was doing the right thing.

'Nothing can be resolved this way.' Jaysee said in a voice that lacked it's normal vigour, 'we don't solve problems by beating at them.'

'That's news to me,' I said 'ever since we met you have been hammering away at me.'

'What do you mean?' Jaysee seemed puzzled by my remark.

'Every call, every call you ever made to my Happy Haven was a series of insults and abuse. I can't remember a single incident that didn't end with you giving me a bollocking.'

He still looked puzzled.

'How does it feel now, Jaysee,' -I was goading him- 'knowing that a light weight wanker can hit back at you?'

My remark was intended to provoke another reaction from him. It succeeded, but not in the way that I had expected.

A smile spread slowly across his features. Just realignment at first, then it became his alligator grin of old. His eyes regained their lustre. He looked his sardonic former self again.

'I may have to revise my opinion of you, Hammond,' he said, 'you have more bottle than I gave you credit for.'

'It would take more than a near punch-up before I would revise my opinion of you.' I said.

'Don't push your luck, Hammond,' he growled, 'just because you have more balls than brains than I gave you credit for it doesn't mean that you are suddenly a good manager.'

'That could be something else you are wrong about, Jaycee,' I said 'because you believe all the reports you get from the computer, you think you have second sight. But the computer gives bum advice, too, you know.'

'That's as may be,' he countered, 'but you can't be a good manager without getting results. The computer just records what you do, after you have done it. Management is about getting it right before it is recorded. And that is something which you have failed to do, Hammond.'

'Even if I did get it right, you wouldn't give me credit for it.'

'If you got it right, Hammond,'-he emphasised if 'I would expect you to do even better. That's what it's all about, always improving. You wouldn't do that if I showered you with praise every time you got something right. You would rest on your laurels instead.'

'How do you think of yourself, Jaycee?' I asked, 'as a lightweight wanker or as God's gift to management.'

'My job is done is when you and all the others do well. Anything that falls short of that is failure.'

'Then why not let us manage in our own way. We don't need Manuals, systems and computers to do it for us. We can think, we can reason, we can judge. And, most important of all, we are there.'

'That' said Jaysee stoutly, 'will never work. We would have hotels all over the country doing their own thing in their own way. It would be impossible. We do not have managers with enough muscle and nous to even consider it.'

'Are you afraid, Jaysee,' I said 'that it might work? It could put you out of a job, you know.'

'You don't have enough bottle or balls to even try it.' I added.

Jaysee was back in control again when he said;

'That will be the day when I don't have enough to do! How long could I have left you on your own with a control clerk robbing you blind and a night manager running a private cat house?'

'O.K.' I said, 'so I was wrong about those two. It is a mistake that I will never make again. It is a lesson that I have learned. It won't happen again.'

"No,' Jaysee snarled, 'it won't happen again, you can be damn sure of that. Next time it will be something else that you are not expecting.'

'And I suppose you will tell me about it after it happens again?'

'Not if I can smell it coming, I won't.'

'Another one of your gypsy warnings, Jaysee? Like the one about the bars manager?'

'Always, Hammond' said Jaysee heavily, 'always assume all your staff are bent until they prove that they are not. That way you don't get caught with your pants down.'

'Jaysee,' I said, 'I have 80 staff in my unit. 2 of them have been dishonest. That also means that 78 were always honest. Why tar them with the same brush?'

'Because the damage caused by those two far outweighs the good done by the other 78, that's why.'

He was beginning to bellow again. Warming to his theme of human failings. A subject of enduring passion, which he could back up with impressive statistics .
....' believe you me, Hammond,' he grated 'eventually you will come around to my point of view. You will fall back on systems and methods which are known to work. You will forget all about the milk of human kindness, grab your profits and run away with them whilst you can. And always keep your balls covered or someone will cut them off.'

'Maybe someone else will, Jaysee, but it won't be because I failed to protect myself. Maybe your balls will be cut off by someone who hates your guts enough to do it.'

It seemed a bleak future that Jaysee was painting for me. A long and arduous slog through suspicion, distrust and doubt of colleagues. if that was what management meant, then it was not for me.

I produced the envelope containing my resignation. I handed it to Jaysee.

'What is it?' he asked.

'My resignation.'

'So, Hammond,' his alligator grin spread wide again, 'you have decided to quit. To chuck it all in. To run away from your problems instead of facing them.'

'I have decided to resign, Jaysee,' I said, 'which is not quitting.'

'Come off it!' he jeered, 'you are much too young to resign for personal or health reasons. You are quitting because you are beaten and you haven't got the guts to see it through to the end.'

'The reasons are my own. I don't have to take any more of this crap from you or anyone else. I resign because I want out. Not for any other reason that you may dream up.'

An unusual silence followed my remark. Jaysee was thrown off his course. He seemed bemused by the turn the debate had taken.

'It's what you wanted all along, Jaysee, isn't it?'

'You have got it all wrong,' he replied, ' I have never wanted you to leave.' He shrugged as he spoke.

'I don't buy that,' I said, 'why all the pressure if you wanted me to stay?'

'What pressure?' He was genuinely perplexed.

'Come on,' I said, 'you leaned on me hard enough to push an elephant over.'

'You are wrong, Hammond, completely wrong.' he replied, 'I treat you and all the other unit managers exactly the same. If there is something wrong in your unit, I point it out to you. That isn't leaning.'

'Hammond,' he continued 'you have a persecution mania. if you want to resign because you can't cope, that's OK by me. But don't use me as your excuse. If you can't cope, just say so and piss off.'

'The only thing around here that I cannot cope with, Jaysee, is you. That is because you are a complete asshole and working really hard to become an even greater asshole.'

Jaysee did not fall into the trap of losing his cool a second time. He grinned at me instead.

'In that case,' he said, 'you can take this back.'

He shoved my resignation back into my pocket.

'But why?' I asked, 'why?'

'Because your stay with Happy Havens is not yet over,' said Jaysee, smoothing the lapels of my jacket, 'for some reason only known to himself, Sir wants to see you.'

'Sir? Sir who wants to see me. Why?'

'Sir' said Jaysee patiently, 'is Walter J Lewis, Chairman and Chief Executive Officer of this group of companies. Lord High Seigneur of all that he surveys, owner and sole proprietor of my body and soul and, as of now, of yours too.'

Jaysee turned his attention to my tie. A gentle twist aligned it to his satisfaction. He took a step back to admire his handiwork.

'But why does he want to see me?' I did not recognise the voice that said it, but it must have been my own.

'Why?' said Jaysee, 'why? Nobody asks Walter why in this organisation. He just tells you when. Which is right now in your case. As soon as I have finished with you. I will ring his secretary and tell her that you are on your way.'

He stood back to admire his valet skills. Still smiling at a joke I did not share.

'Just give me a few moments before you do that, Jaysee.' Please.' I added.

Jaysee nodded brusquely. 'Five minutes, then.'

It was as close to compassion as he could possibly go. The roar from the office rose and fell away as he left the room.

I had never felt more alone in my life, standing there in an empty room next to the operations powerhouse. I was isolated from colleagues with commitment, a maverick who did not share the common aim. The only swimmer going upstream against the current.

I think it was a combination of curiosity and fatalism that prompted me seek out Walter in his lair.

Just like a pupil summoned from Junior School by the Headmaster, I did not run eagerly. In fact every movement towards my next meeting increased my sense of impending doom.

CHAPTER 23 REFORM

Power, authority and organisation clout cannot defy the laws of gravity. They must flow downhill. The higher the fountain head, the thinner the trickle in the foothills. When the stream reaches the hotels of a group, it's force is spent. The unit manager carries responsibility, but he lacks authority.

And unit managers, the lowest common denominator spear chuckers in the hierarchy, must answer to their lords and masters for all their misdeeds.

Walter, Lord High Chairman and C.E.O of Happy Haven Hotels Inc. lived in the rarefied atmosphere of the 32nd floor, the symbolic peak of the organisation pinnacle.

From this vantage point, he had become aware of a disturbance in the foothills. He had focused his sharp stare onto me, enjoying all the advantages that height gives to the observer.

I was ushered into his opulent office by a deferential secretary. She introduced me as 'Mr Martin Hammond.'

She had told me in the outer office that 'The Chairman always likes to know the Christian name of his guests.' She had also told me that she didn't know why he wanted to see me.

'Sit down, Martin, sit down' he said, 'I'll be with you in just a moment.'

A pleasant, avuncular greeting from a man who was much smaller than I expected him to be. His Black Country accent was pronounced, his goatee beard was distinguished and his presence seemed to fill the room.

'I'll be right with you,' he said cheerfully 'just a few letters to sign.'

He scanned the letters in a leather folder briefly. He nodded several times and had a brief conversation with his secretary which I did not hear. When he had signed all the letters she left quietly.

The door clicked shut behind her.

Sir came bobbing over towards me, smiling and effusive. He sat in the broad leather chair opposite mine. He beamed goodwill.

'I expect you are wondering why I asked to see you?'

'Yes, Sir' I said, 'I did wonder.'

'I would like to meet all the managers,' he said 'but I just do not have enough time -they are always too busy to see me.'

He leaned across a low table between us confidentially and tapped my knee.

I laughed nervously as the thought crossed my mind that he might be gay.

'Shall we have some tea?' Walter asked suddenly 'or would you prefer something stronger?' He was poised on the edge of his chair. He looked ready to retrieve something.

'Tea will be just fine, Sir,' I said.

'It will be here in just a moment,' he said, 'I ordered it when Miss Forbes was in here.'

'Well now, Martin,' he said, leaning back in his chair, 'I seem to be hearing your name mentioned a great deal recently. What have you done to deserve such popularity?'

'It is not popularity,' I replied. 'everyone in Head Office has been using me for target practice recently.'

'You can draw attention to yourself ' Walter said, 'by being very good at your job or very bad at it. if you stay in the middle you are never noticed.'

'I don't think I have enough brownie points to be in the first category,' I said, 'so it must be the second.'

'That can happen, Martin' he said 'but it doesn't have to mean that you are always in the wrong.'

'I don't understand that Sir.' I said.

Walter stroked his beard thoughtfully.

'In a group of hotels like this,' he waved around the compass points, 'everything has to be standardised. Every time a guest arrives in one of our hotels, he must find everything he has been led to expect. We have more than 12,000 guests every night and we set out to cater for all their needs and wants.'

Stated with Black Country emphasis, it seemed most credible.

'Naturally,' he continued, 'there will always be some guests who are upset by this standardisation. Equally true, there will always be some managers who resist because it takes the initiative away from them.'

'If these managers stand up to be counted, they will be noticed.'

'Tell me,' I asked 'what usually happens to those who stand up to be counted?'.
'Walter replied.'We listen very carefully to what they say.'

'And after you have listened. What happens then?'

'We need to be very sure about their motives,' Walter said, 'then we decide what to do.'

He spoke softly in reply to my question. So softly that it made me feel uncomfortable.

The arrival of the teatray was a welcome diversion. Over tea, in a conversational way, I said;
'I am surprised that it is so easy to see you. I would have expected to find a battery of secretaries and a waiting list a mile long between the Chairman and a casual visitor.'

Walter smiled impishly. His appearance was deceiving. He did not look like the accepted image of a modern captain of industry. He lacked the stature and the gravitas, distinction and bearing of higher profile role models. But on the scale which starts with featherweight and ends with heavyweight, he was way up top. Handle very carefully came across loud and clear.

'It is a popular illusion, Martin,' he confided 'that Chairmen are busy people who don't have a moment to spare. It is a myth, of course, because you don't become Chairman unless you are very good at delegating to other people. I am so good at delegating,' he leaned forward and tapped my knee again, 'that I have virtually nothing to do all day except talk to people.'

I began to worry about the knee tapping.

'How often?' he asked 'have you telephoned this office and asked to speak to me?'

'Never,' I said, a little too quickly.

'Neither does anyone else. Except those who have complaints to make. They always seem to get through all right.'

'Everybody else seems to be very busy all the time.' I ventured.

'That' he replied 'is because I am very good at my job.'

He smiled as he spoke. But the set of his face made his words very believable. Behind that *bonhomie*, concealed by courtesy, there was an iron fist barely covered by a velvet glove. I was still not sure why I was there. Nothing that had been said so far had shed any light or explained why I was there in Walter's office.

I was treading warily when I said;

'You have probably seen my name on several Green Copies recently.'

'Yes' agreed Walter, 'I have. Six, is'nt it?'

That shattered the myth about the avuncular Chairman with nothing to do all day long. The output of Green Copies in this treadmill must have taken at least two hours each day to read.

'I'll let you into a secret, Martin, provided that you promise not to tell anyone else.'

I agreed. Cautiously, still on guard.

'When I was a young man, I used to manage hotels, just as you do.. To be honest, I don't think I was very good at it. I was sacked three times for not toeing the line. At the time, I thought that my bosses were wrong because I was full of bright ideas about how to do things better. With hindsight, I can see that they were right and I was wrong. It was only because I was so sure of myself that I started this company with borrowed money.'

'But do you know, Martin, what I set out to do?'

I shook my head.

'I wanted to run the best hotel in town, with the best service in the world, at a price that everyone could afford. It turned out to be a pipe dream, it couldn't be done economically. But see what came out of it, Martin, in today's terms. The determination to provide the best at an affordable price is always right, and I had a gut feeling that it could be done. And I worked at it until it came right, which took many, many years.'

'As a result of that experience, Martin,' he said 'I can forgive a man almost anything that he has done, provided that he has done it with commitment.'

'But money and wealth must have motivated you, surely?, I asked .

Walter shook his head slowly from side to side,

'It is not, and never was, about money. It is about knowing what people want even before they know it themselves. And providing it. Profit follows from providing a service. The pursuit of profit for it's own sake is never worthwhile. Profit is just a gauge to show how good your service is.'
'
'And luck,' I asked, 'did luck playa part in your growth?'

'You can be lucky or unlucky - either way it shouldn't affect your plans. You can't rely on luck, it comes and it goes. What is much more important than luck is persistence. That is something you can control. The finishing quality in a man is much more important than his luck. Provided that he sticks at it, he will succeed in the end.'

'But surely,' I said, 'there is nothing to be gained by sticking at the wrong job?'

'That's true,' Walter said 'but your own judgment should tell you when to give in which is the 59th second of the 59th minute before the irrevocable deadline. Then you pick yourself up, dust yourself down and start all over again.'

The time had come to clarify a few things. Walter had settled in his chair. He seemed to be enjoying a comfortable chat about his past, his present job and his outlook on life within the Happy Haven Empire. He was a most amiable and avuncnlar companion, apparently free from any social or commercial pressure to come to the point.

But there could be no doubt about the reason for my presence in Head Office. I had been summoned to appear before my masters. To explain, to justify, to excuse, to apologise. I had chosen to defy, to insult, to upset, to attack.

Everyone else believed me to be guilty of the most heinous crime known to the organisation -the crime of being different. Yet when I came into the den of the Lord High Executioner, he told me stories of his past and asked me to keep secrets. He had also revealed a penchant for tapping my knees that was very disturbing.

The time had come, I decided, to change the conversation from the general to the specific.

'Did you know that I came here to-day to resign from Happy Havens?'

'I know that you offered your resignation to my District Manager.'

'Then why,' I asked 'did you bother to see me?'

'I have several reasons,' he said enigmatically, ' top of the list is the reason why you want to leave.'

'Not to talk me out of it?' I asked.

'The act is important to you, Martin, the reason is important to me.'

He waited, patiently, for me to begin.

I gave my version of a unit manager's lot. It was the truth as I saw it. , ... when we manage your hotels for you, it is to the exclusion of everything else in our lives. From dawn to dusk, and even through the night, seven days a week, 52 weeks a year we are there, tending a machine which never stops. O.K., you do get some sleep and you can get away on leave sometimes but you can't relax because there are problems building up all the time. It is like sitting on a keg of dynamite, waiting for it to blow up.'

'if that sounds like a whinge, it is'nt. If we couldn't do it, we would have run away long ago. It is not the sharp end that causes the problems. It is Head

Office. Personally, I enjoy the job down at the sharp end. But the bit that really pisses me off is the form filling, the returns, the questionnaires, the flying visits from Head Office, the advisors, the so called experts, all demanding instant attention.'

'And what do you get in return for all this Head Office attention? A fistful of meaningless statistics and a mouthful of abuse. Both of which you can manage without.'

'To-day,' I said, 'was the end of my war with your Head Office. I have had a run-in with Legal and Secretarial, Personnel, Accounts, Management Development and my District Manager. I handed out a lot of advice that was not accepted. I came within an ace of a punch-up, too.'

'It was probably,' I said 'the most enjoyable day since I first joined. But I can't stay with the company. Too many bosses have me on their short list for the heave-ho.'

I felt easier after my outburst, as if I had talked a burden off my back. I had vowed that my last day with Happy Havens would be memorable. It was a bonus that I had managed to take a snap shot at Walter to add to the other targets of the day.

Walter had allowed me to continue without interruption, comment, question or emotion. If he had any feelings at all, they did not show. He sat back in his chair, relaxed and comfortable.

For a long time after I finished, he just looked pensive. Then he said;

'All managers are volunteers, Martin. No one presses them into service. They can step off any time they want to. The decision to become a manager is a personal one, and, God knows, we have made mistakes with appointments and promotions. When managers volunteer their services, we have no way of knowing what level of leadership they possess or how they will stand up to pressure. We can only find that out by shoving them in the deep end. '

'But' he said firmly, 'this much I do know. It is the finishing quality, not the killer instinct, which determines how far managers will go in my company.'

'If a manager,' he stated 'has the strength to finish his job and sacrifices some sensitivity on the way, he is better at his job after that. If he has to make tough decisions, he will not be loved for it. But he should not be despised either, for it takes courage to see it through to the end.'

'A wise man,' Walter said, 'knows that there will always be a loser in every competition. Only a fool will make excuses for himself.'

There was a message in there somewhere. It wasn't crystal clear, but it applied to me.

'How do you classify me, then? As a runner-up who didn't win or as a starter who did not finish.'

'I never classify people, Martin,' he replied, 'you can't put people into pigeon holes and expect them to behave predictably.'

'The only label that I have put on you so far,' he added, 'is unusual.'

'What is unusual about me,' I said 'is that I have questioned the need for a Head Office to dump problems on me. I can find more than enough to do every day without them. They don't make my job easier, they don't produce anything. They look at what I have done, after I have done it and tell me to do it in a different way. They shove Manuals at me and say; Read this and learn it by heart. Then do it.'

'If we really knew what has to be done in the hotels,' Walter said, 'we wouldn't need Manuals. They are for guidelines only. The Manual is not a substitute for judgment and thought. That is what we expect from managers, that is why they are there.'

'Jaysee said much the same sort of thing,' I said 'but he used different words. He said 'you are a light-weight wanker without the wit or nous to organise a piss-up for publicans.'

I had hoped that blunt words would shake him off his diplomatic perch and cause some reaction. I was disappointed.

'Martin' he said' my Head Office is in the same position as any team manager.'
'We can only influence the game before it begins. After the off you are on your own, we can't do anything about it then. You have to do the best you can with the resources that you have. After the game is over, it is natural to talk about it and tease

out improvements. That is what my Head Office is all about.'

'That is fine in theory,' I said, 'but you expect us to win every time. Even if we do win, you still say we didn't win by a big enough margin.'

'And do you think, Martin,' he said 'that we should encourage people to give less than their best?'

I had to agree with him. Anything else was suicide.

'You are right about that.' I said.

'So do you still think of my Head Office as an unnecessary burden for you to carry?'
'I don't have to think about it any more,' I said, 'this my last day here.' I produced my resignation from my pocket. I placed it on the table between us.

If the gesture made any impact, it did not show. Walter stared at me steadily, inscrutable as the Sphinx, with unmoved granite features.

'All your problems, Martin,' he said 'come about because you channel your energy into questioning the rules of the game. You think that the rules are unfair because it does not suit you to stick to them.'

Walter's comment was perceptive enough to make me feel really uncomfortable.

His expression had changed subtly. The avuncular, friendly manner was still evident, but there was a steely undertone to his words that struck chill.

I tried to match his stare. I could think of nothing to say which sounded either brave or sensible. He leaned forward and tapped my knee. A quick, deft movement.

'You are shouting against thunder. You will never be heard. It is a competition that you cannot win, either here or anywhere else.'

He leaned back in his chair and pulled his beard thoughtfully.
 It was more from a desire to have the last word than from conviction that I said;

'You are probably right. But I have nothing to lose, and everything to gain if you are wrong. Maybe I am not the Happy Haven type. Maybe I never did have a future with you.'

'In this company, Martin,' he said drily 'you make your own future.'
'I am always on the look-out for managers with special qualities,' Walter said, 'one of which is the ability to question why we do things this way or that.'

My curiosity level took off. It was impossible to ignore such temptation. He had me intrigued. I was drawn back into his web by invisible elastic.

'What special qualities are you referring to?' I asked.

'It is impossible to define,' Walter said ' but I know that some men possess this quality and others do not. You cannot see it, feel it, touch it or smell it.

290

But you know when it is there. It is a combination of things that does not show in his face, manner or attitude.'

'Then how do you recognise it?'

'The results tell half of the story. The other half emerges in hundreds of tiny details in the Weekly Report.'

Another fable blew up in my face. The one about all that paper just being filed. Walter was a very busy man indeed if he spent his time reading all the Weekly Reports and the Green Copies.

'You read all those reports?' I asked incredulously.

'Every single one of them,' he replied, 'every one tells a story.'

I let out a long, slow whistle. If there was a gallantry award for reading boring stories, then Walter should win it.

'What happens then?' I asked.

'I meet with my Management team. We discuss the results achieved. Then we decide what to do. After that the District Managers talk to the unit managers. You know what happens after that, don't you, Martin?'

Several pieces of a jigsaw puzzle fell into place with a loud clonk in my mind. A complete, and a new picture emerged.- distinct, clear images of a purposeful organisation pursuing Walter's dream of the best at an affordable price. Which could only be achieved by strict control in the hotels where nearly all the money was spent.

By the unit manager, who else? I recalled some of the abuse hurled at me by Jaysee in the past. With hind-sight, I conld see that some of it was justified. An acid twinge of regret began to burn inside me.

'What,' I asked 'are you going to do about that?' I pointed to the envelope lying on the table between us. 'It's my resignation.'

A long, fraught silence followed.

'Yes', said Walter, 'I know what it is.'

'Well?' I think I was holding my breath when I said it.

'When managers resign from my company, Martin,' Walter said, 'it is usually because they have a better job to go to. Then I congratulate them, wish them well and tell them to stay in touch with me. Where are you off to?'

The tension mounted as I tried to think of a suitable reply. I couldn't match Walter for calm and control. It probably showed.

'Nowhere' I blurted out, 'I haven't got another job to go to.'

'Then what do you expect to gain by resigning?' Walter asked, turning the knife in the wound.

I had found it much easier to tell Jaysee why I wanted out because we were eyeball to eyeball at the time. I can find the right words when I am uptight. It is not so easy for me to find good reasons during a calm debate.

'It seemed like a good idea at the time,' I said lamely.

Walter looked at me in contempt.

'The time to leave a job, Martin, is when there is nothing more for a manager to do. Have you reached that stage yet?'

'No, of course not. There is plenty to be done yet'.

Walter's voice had the granite edge back again when he said;

'I want you to remember four things, Martin, and don't ever forget them. They are the Golden Rules for all managers in this group.'

He held up his right hand. The index finger was raised.

'One. the time to resign is when the job is done. Never before.'

'Two' Another finger went up. 'Never make a promise you don't intend to keep.'

'Three.' Three fingers lined up. 'Never make a threat you don't intend to carry out.'

'Four.' All his fingers made a wall.' Never start something you don't intend to finish.'

'Remember these rules, son, and you and I will always see eye to eye.'

Then, very deliberately, he tore my resignation in half. I was preparing a short speech of thanks when he said;

'You have a job of work to do, Martin, back in your Happy Haven. Get it done. Get it right. Then I have another job for you to do.'

'Where?' I asked, still catching up with events.

'I'll let you know when the time comes.' he replied, 'it will probably be away from UK. We are looking at proposition in East Europe, India, Russia, Mainland China and South America. I've got you earmarked for one of them.'

'When?'

'When your Happy Haven is the best there is.'

'Boss', I said, 'I think I owe you an apology for being wrong about a lot of things.'

'It's accepted.' he said briskly 'now we both have jobs to get on with, haven't we?'

****

I had reached the door of Walter's office when a half hidden thought surfaced without any prompting. It concerned something from the past, a bit of unfinished business that needed to be tidied up and put to rest.

I turned to face Walter. He was standing with his back to the window, framed by the setting sun.

'By the way, Boss,' I said 'do you know a girl called Naomi Dwight?'

His face was bland and relaxed. He answered without hesitation.

'Yes. I know her. Do you?'

That was another one of Walter's surprising responses. He seemed to catch me off guard every time. I had planned a terrible revenge for Naomi's former lover. Now that I was face to face with him I didn't know what to do.
Walter looked at me steadily, amused by something.
'Well ....' I said, 'well, we are engaged to be married, you know.'

'Congratulations,' he said' you have made an excellent choice. When is the wedding.?'

Another disconcerting question from Walter the unpredictable.

'I, er, I haven't asked her yet.' I said.

'Let me know when she says Yes, Martin.' he said warmly.

'You will be the second person to know,' I replied.

'Send me an invitation, Martin,' he said cheerfully, 'I love weddings.'

I got ready to leave after nodding agreement. I was almost at the door when his voice commanded my attention.

'One more thing, Martin!.' All the apprehension came flooding back. I tensed up again.
'Yes?'

'Don't forget to order the wedding cake, will you?' I relaxed. We both laughed at a passing good joke. When the laughter died down I got ready to leave again.

'Boss,' I said, 'you are full of surprises.'

We exchanged conspirator's smiles. Both of us were sure that we knew more about the other's mettle by now.

Chapter 24. Recuperation.

I drove back to my Happy Haven very slowly, glad to be alone and uninterrupted. There was much to think about. It had been a very busy day.

One day in a lifetime does not make you much older. But these last few hours had made me much wiser. An enduring wisdom which would last a lifetime. There were many lessons to be absorbed, many new concepts to be taken on board. And quite a few of the old ones to be chucked overboard, too.

I have charged into Head Office like a lion, spoiling for a fight. I had come out like a lamb, somehow converted into a company man.

In reality, there wasn't a great deal of difference between Jaysee's message and Walter's message. Both had said much the same sort of thing -do it my way-The difference lay in the style. Jaysee had tried to ram it down my throat. Walter had sold me on the idea of competing within the rules.

Walter had converted me, by some evangelical magic, into the kind of company man that I would have despised yesterday. And it was going to be all uphill from this point on. I had made some new and powerful enemies in Head Office to-day and I would have to work with them much more closely in the future. Some of the comments I had made were bound to back-fire. Jaysee would be even tougher than before.

'Never start something you don't intend to finish.' Walter had given that as Rule number four.

'O.K., Boss,' I said out loud. 'it's a deal!'

The driver of the car alongside mine in the traffic jam assumed that I was swearing at him. He made a rude gesture.

I blew him a huge kiss. He sped off into the gathering gloom.

Alone and driving carefully on automatic pilot I had time to consider the enormity of the task that I had set for myself. Deep down in my gut, I knew that I intended to become a company man who complied with all four Golden Rules of engagement. Just like any other soldier/spearchucker I had to toe the line and obey my bosses and all those who were further up the pay scale.

But not wholly without the occasional kick-back. Walter had made it abundantly clear to me that he approved of those who challenged the status quo occasionally and with justification. But I had to forego the luxury of aggressive reaction to all semblance of command from above. It was an instinctive reaction that I had assumed could be regarded as a hallmark of confidence, amusing and acceptable behaviour to all. That was just one of the beliefs that I had to jettison in the new acceptance of the corporate style which substituted uniformity for self expression. I would have to learn a new way of expressing myself to others. Another formidable task to add to the list of mandatory changes before Martin Hammond, Mark 2 could be re-born.

The drive back to my Happy Haven was definitely a seminal journey for me. It did lack the thunder and lightning of Saint Paul's Road to Damascus drama, but I had to accept that my life had changed direction suddenly. I was going back to the scene of a management failure which was already beginning to haunt me. I wondered if Walter (who had out-thought and outwitted me several times in a relatively short time frame) had done this deliberately to emphasise or test my resolve.
That was just one of those issues that I did not expect to hear about, ever.
It would have been much easier for me if Walter had sent me to a new patch where I could start all over again without the impediment from past mistakes to burden me.
So how did Walther's 4 Golden Rules apply to me now?
Resignation was out of the question. Walther had made it quite clear to me that my resignation was not the solution to neither his nor my dilemma. I had to prove myself amidst the chaos and disorder of my Happy Haven (my own handiwork) by becoming "the best there is" amongst equals with identical tasks. That sounded like a Herculean task which would demand pragmatic and creative thinking to even begin an improving trend. I needed to recruit immediately a new Bars Manager, a new permanent Night Manager and a new Comptroller. I was not looking for replacement staff. I needed new on-side team players with the right skills who were honest. diligent and willing to join a team with long term ambitions to succeed.

When these priority appointments were made I could lead a winning team of colleagues who could work with, assist and encourage my other loyal team leaders whose conduct at all times had been beyond reproach. If there was a glaring fault to be found, it was my own failure to lead, support and encourage them enough. Pinky and Perky, Chef, Ethel, Iceberg and 75 others had all deserved better from me.

The next 2 Golden rules were about carrying out threats and promises. They seemed to warn about the perils of not doing enough to plan your future activities wisely and being foolish enough to utter words which were not the result of deep thought and judgement. I needed to work very hard on that to succeed in becoming a better manager without behaving like an unaccountable politician.

And that left Golden Rule no 4. – Never start something you don't intend to finish – as a catch all which called on all the planning and expertise associated with the other rules, but on a scale of intensity which relied on years and years of experience of both success and failure. My experience of both was growing exponentially and could always be broadened by consultation. But my basic instincts told me that this missing piece of the jig-saw was gifted to some and denied to others, irrespective of culture education or exposure. Walther was seeking the handful of young people who had this instinctive and precious gift and had been unable to demonstrate it so far. It would be the ultimate compliment if Walther had somehow concluded that he had seen the seeds of the entrepreneur in me and was giving me the chance to prove that he was right.

That was all the motivation I needed to nail my flag to Walther's mast.

I could kill two birds with one stone. Walther and I could be the joint winners who took the top prize.

My journey glided on towards my Happy Haven in peaceful co-existence with other commuting drivers. A swift summary of progress to date would state "The who, the what, the where and the when were in plain sight". Together they made up a daunting mountain to climb. The "how" was not as easily defined and contained all the doubts.

I had set out earlier in the same day to confront all my perceived tormentors in Head Office with the avowed intention of wreaking revenge on all of them according to their just desserts.
I could not say that my mission had been successful as no truly apparent change had been achieved. I had made some new enemies who would no doubt let me know in the near future just how miffed they were by our meetings on their patch. That was just another one of the "how" problems to be faced in the future. They were bruised and a little battered. I was bloody and unbowed but feeling very insecure and sought after for the wrong reasons. That did not reflect a draw – it was more like a contest lost on points scored.

I had also made the mistake of telling several of my colleagues that I was going to Head Office spoiling for a fight and that I might not come back to the hotel other than to collect the few slender possessions that made up all my worldly goods and chattels. With 20/20 hindsight that had turned out to be another mistake which would call for an explanation that I had not yet constructed. (Walther Golden rule 3)

So I steeled myself ready for the grand return to my Happy Haven. I could not expect a chorus of "Hail the conquering hero comes" when I arrived back to confront my colleagues. The best that I could hope for would be a deafening silence and a chance to justify my sins of omission and commission.

My automatic route finding return to my Happy Haven was completed when I joined the neon lit filter lane that directed all guests to Happy Havens Reception and Car Park. A deeply buried instinct told me that it was already a busy night in progress – the car park was crowded-.

I dismissed the cowardly thought that I could slip into my office via the back door. I marched through the swing doors with all my insecurity masked by a confident stride.

Ethel was the first to see me. She waved and beckoned me towards Reception. We exchanged affectionate smiles.

'Miss Tammond' she said 'I 'ave a message for you from 'ead Office.'

Without waiting for a reply from me she said;

'Miss Forbes, secretary to Chairmen and C.E.O. at 'ead office rang to say that you were on your way back and should arrive at about 6.30 p.m.'

She gave a mock salute with widespread fingers and stood approximately to attention.

'I fink he was worried about you?'

'Thank you, Ethel' I said as a tsunami of relief and doubt was flushed away from my thoughts.

'I will be in my office if I am needed.'

Walther had demonstrated his support for both me and my command in a striking and considerate way. He had endorsed me to all the staff here in a way that left no doubt about his intention to reinforce my leadership. And he had done so in a unique way that only he could bestow on a trusted colleague. No other endorsement carried that amount of clout. I had no doubt that Ethel had relayed his message to all on duty that evening. In one brief stroke he had left me with no long winded apology to offer my crew who had been made aware of his continuing support for Martin Hammond.

Yet again, Walther had out-witted and out-guessed me and read my thoughts without even being in contact. He went up several more notches in my esteem.

I decided that a celebration was needed. To mark the launch of Martin Hammond, Born again company man. The guest list should include all the loyal colleagues who had stood by me in the past.

All the people at my Happy Haven who had never let me down, who had been constant and supportive. Pinky. Perky. Ethel. Chef. Iceberg .... the list was as long as the payroll. It would be a staff party, I decided, for all of them. Plus a few specially invited guests, like Louis.

But even more than that celebration, I yearned for the special kind of love, solace, comfort and support that could only be found in the bosom of Naomi-Naomi Dwight. I longed to let her know what sort of day I had endured and the conclusions that I had reached for us both. And I had a proposal to put to her. I tried to imagine her response. I did not succeed.

END

www.ingramcontent.com/pod-product-compliance
Lightning Source LLC
Chambersburg PA
CBHW051800170526
45167CB00005B/1813